A Fire in the Forest

Religious Life in Ireland

Edited by Michael J. Breen
Survey by John A. Weafer

VERITAS

First published 2001 by
Veritas Publications
7/8 Lower Abbey Street
Dublin 1
Ireland

Email publications@veritas.ie
Website www.veritas.ie

ISBN 1 85390 534 8

A catalogue record for this book is available from the British Library.

Cover design by Colette Dower
Cover photograph © Imagefile
Printed in the Republic of Ireland by Betaprint Ltd, Dublin

Veritas books are printed on paper made from the wood pulp of managed forests. For every tree felled, at least one tree is planted, thereby renewing natural resources.

For we religious live a style of life which goes against the culture of affluence and instant gratification. For the immediacy of the love of another we seek to be found by the dazzling darkness of divine love; for the status of wealth and possession we follow the One who had nowhere to lay his head; for the independence and adventure of following all our own potential we promise obedience to our superiors. We live often as folk foolish, our eyes fixed on a star mocked by others.

In all this we share the life of the One who calls us. When all is prayed and done, the symbol of our true ministry is the cross. Only in Calvary do we find the true meaning of sacrifice: body given, love suffering even beyond what we might imagine. Maybe at a moment of darkest suffering we have shared the experience of Jesus who knew resurrection in the depths of death. Can we now be people who proclaim by word and lifestyle that the fruit of death is resurrection, that no Christian or human striving for God can bypass the suffering of the cross?

Adapted from an unpublished letter by a religious
to a candidate on the eve of ordination

Contents

Foreword

There is a move currently afoot to have St Columbanus declared a co-patron of Europe. His contribution to religious life alone, in such places as Luxeuil, Bregenz, St Gallen and Bobbio, has made him richly deserving of the title. At the age of 50 he set out from the famous monastery of Bangor to become a missionary pilgrim for Christ.

The history of religious life in Ireland in the intervening 1400 years has had its ups and downs. Nevertheless, the charisma has survived because it depended not on human means but rather on the indomitable energy of the Holy Spirit. I welcome this report, which contains the findings of a research project undertaken on behalf of the Conference of Religious of Ireland. Its accurate and up-to-date statistical information on religious personnel working and living in Ireland today makes it valuable and interesting.

In this report, congregational leaders identify the most important trends in religious life. They tell of their concerns and their hopes. The great majority are either enthusiastic or hopeful towards religious life. The main hope is to remain faithful to the charisma and live it vibrantly and creatively.

I think it is worth recalling what exactly the charisma of every religious is – to dedicate oneself totally to God, by an act of supreme love, in a sacred promise, for the honour and service of God. So the religious is totally dedicated and supremely committed to the highest cause possible – the religious is special indeed. It is important never to forget that no matter what the challenges may be.

I was thrilled to read of one man who said: 'I consider that these are exciting times to be a religious and I am not at all despondent. Christianity was never a "mass" religion and has always achieved far more in the hearts and minds of people when it was forced into the role of underdog and identified with the poor, the vulnerable and the marginalised'. Quite true, just as religious life is always seen as a lifestyle counter-cultural to that of the majority.

No doubt Irish religious will continue to challenge and surprise as they have done throughout history. For a way of life rooted in love and open to complete self-dedication to God, in solidarity with the oppressed, is always going to appeal to high-minded and generous people.

It is encouraging to hear that Irish religious have, in recent times, moved to respond to unmet needs of people who are homeless, unemployed and disadvantaged. New beginnings, often unnoticed, multiply. The faith and joy, which fill this report, signal an unmistakable Pentecost.

✠ Sean Brady
Archbishop of Armagh
14 July 2001

Contributors

Dr Michael J. Breen, a priest of the Archdiocese of Dublin, is Head of the Department of Media and Communication Studies at Mary Immaculate College, University of Limerick.

John A. Weafer is a Social and Religious Researcher with Weafer & Associates Research and Consulting Ltd.

Sr Elizabeth Maxwell PBVM is Secretary General of the Conference of Religious of Ireland (CORI).

Christopher Dillon OSB is Abbot of the Benedictine Abbey in Glenstal, Co Limerick.

Professor Dermot Keogh is Professor of History, University College Cork.

Dr Tony Fahey is Senior Research Officer with the Economic and Social Research Institute (ESRI).

Sr Teresa McCormack PBVM is director of the Education Office, Conference of Religious of Ireland (CORI).

Introduction

1

The Forest is on Fire: A story of birth, growth, decline and renewal

Michael J. Breen

The giant sequoia, *Sequoia sempervirens*, is the tallest tree in the world, growing in excess of 100 metres high, 25 metres in circumference, with a bark up to 1 metre thick. The great sequoia forests of southern California have been threatened with extinction though fire, and great efforts were made in the past to minimise fire in the forests, with extinguishing and control of forest fires a priority. Research, however, has led to an alternative approach to fire management. It now transpires that fire serves a triple purpose in a sequoia forest – it clears the ground for new growth, it opens the canopy, and the ash of the burned trees is the perfect medium for the new seedlings. It transpires that sequoia seed dispersal, seedling establishment, growth, and survival are highest where fires have burned most intensely[1]. As Kilgore puts it, 'in all probability, the giant sequoia survives today because of the role fire played in its life cycle'[2]. A fire in the forest is the harbinger of new growth, new life.

This theme is echoed again and again in this volume, not just in the comments of the congregational leaders who generated the raw data for the report, but also in the reflections of the various commentators who responded to the invitation of CORI to write about religious life in Ireland in the context of the report.

The volume is divided into two sections. The first is the substantial report by John Weafer: 'Profile of Religious in Ireland' (1999). This research was commissioned by CORI as a follow-up to a previous survey from 1989-90. It should be noted that the data here refers only to active apostolic religious; it does not include information on contemplatives or missionary societies.

There has been rapid and profound change in Ireland in the last ten years in which the Church has been involved. At a time of economic boom, religious orders have had fewer recruits. The impact on religious life has been significant – fewer men and women, an ageing profile, profound changes in ministries. It was deemed essential to document such changes.

When this report was received at CORI, a decision was made that it should be published, and that such publication should be accompanied by a series of reflections that would represent a variety of perspectives. The change in religious life can be seen through a variety of lenses, particularly the two opposing lenses of decline vs. transformation. The decision to publish the material is a bold statement by CORI about the future of religious life and a strong assertion of the transformation model over that of decline.

There are some who speak of the crisis in religious life today. They are absolutely correct, in an entirely literal sense. There are certainly signs of a crisis, one that has become more acute in the last decade. But the root meaning of the term crisis is important here – a crisis is an opportunity, properly defined as a stage in a sequence of events at which the trend of all future events is determined. In terms of religious life, the upheaval being faced is surely a crisis; it is neither necessarily good nor bad. We do indeed live in changing times, when old certainties have been lost, new doubts are raised, and the future sometimes appears quite uncertain. But these changes are not signs of immanent death.

John Weafer's report provides a mass of detail which will present hours of joy to quantitative sociologists who may wish to pore over the figures. Some things jump out at once – the numbers of older religious, the growth of religious communities (from 1,136 in 1970 to 1,838 in 1999) as smaller communities are established, the wide variety of ministries, the decline in teaching religious at both primary and secondary level (3,640 in 1989 to 1,262 in 1999), and the growth in social services and pastoral ministries.

Within the data, interesting pictures emerge. It is clear that religious life is certainly different, that the numbers of sisters, brothers and priests will be less than heretofore. Numbers have decreased when compared to the heyday of the '50s and '60s. But, as Tony Fahey indicates elsewhere in this volume, there were 200 nuns in Ireland in 1800 and 1500 by 1851. Decreases in numbers are relative and the base against which such decreases are measured is clearly important. There is, of course, more to the figures than decrease.

These raw figures are given a context in the following chapter on 'Trends in Religious Life'. The major trends identified by the Congregational Leaders are solidarity with the poor, collaboration, justice, and spirituality. Allied to these are concerns about ageing profiles, management issues and new expressions of religious charisms. Particularly striking is the chord of hope, where, interestingly enough, increase in vocations are joint fifth after fidelity to charism, renewal of passion and values, collaboration, and identification of new needs.

This is further amplified with some 91 expressions of positive feelings (25 on new life emerging, 21 on the need for religious life, 13 on God calling, 13 on joy, 11 on necessity of renewal) toward religious life as opposed to 22 negative expressions (10 on concern with ageing and 10 on confusion in transition). Ninety-two per cent of congregational leaders express their conviction that religious life has a future in Ireland.

The statistics indicate a strong belief in religious life despite the difficulties of the present age. Such positive expression is, as Dermot Keogh puts it, 'a prediction rooted in hope rather than a mere aspiration ... the responses do not betray any sense of hopelessness.'

The second section of the volume deals with data from differing points of view. Elizabeth Maxwell, secretary-general of CORI, responds to the figures by drawing on her own extensive knowledge of, and respect for, religious men and women in Ireland. She deals with the willingness of the active religious congregations to adapt in relation to their ministries, something already well underway. But she also points out that religious life is defined not by ministry but by the interior life, and that 'success will be measured by fidelity.'

She touches on the attribution of the current decline in numbers by some to the scandals and revelations of the 1990s, rejecting such an analysis as facile. The downturn in numbers of recruits became evident in 1970. Those scandals have had an impact on morale and congregational leaders must find a way of addressing this where necessary. She also reflects on what community might mean in contemporary terms, as a new definition is sought of what a 'union of minds and hearts entails.'

Christopher Dillon further elaborates this theme in his chapter on *Vita Consecrata*. What is at issue in religious life is 'the beauty of God, shown in the life of Christ and visible, today, in the life of his dedicated disciples.' He situates this in part with the preferential option for the poor, the disadvantaged and the marginalised, reminding us of some groups who fill these categories today: the aged, the sick, refugees. Of particular relevance is his point that society rapidly realises that the public purse is inadequate to the needs of service that has been supplied by Christian dedication.

The need for witness is evident today: 'The innate value of this life needs to be proclaimed, not so much by speaking about it as by allowing its holiness to shine through the lived example of communities and individuals; but by communities, rather than by individuals.' He believes that it is this very visible commitment that truly speaks volumes about religious life and what it entails.

Dermot Keogh looks at the data from the historical perspective and pulls no punches: 'the conclusions that must be drawn ought to have a sobering effect on both members of religious orders and lay Catholics alike.' He asks 'why and how do religious congregations find themselves facing the contemporary challenges quantified in the survey' and sets the answer in an historical frame.

As he looks to the future, he offers some excellent advice to all interested in the future of religious life. Worthy of emphasis is his stress on what the future should not be: 'While the modalities of discovering new religious forms is not a subject for this short essay, the embedding of the diverse religious traditions in Irish society will *not* be achieved by the founding of secretive, closed lay groups who form a new elite or elect. One of the most significant dangers facing Irish Catholicism today is the temptation for those in authority to look to 'loyalists' who feel most comfortable working under a cloak of secrecy in order to preserve the future of the Catholic Church.'

Tony Fahey provides a fascinating account of an early conflict between vision and reality in religious life, stating that 'money talks – and even saintly reverend mothers must listen to what it says.' He offers a stimulating critique on the issue of social justice and the lack of systemic social commentary among religious congregations in the Catholic Church. He raises the challenge of economic prosperity amongst religious congregations and their consequent freedom to move in new directions without constraint, and questions whether founders like Catherine McAuley would support 'the retreat from service to the better off.'

He also looks at the changed world of vocations, where in the past religious life was seen as superior to other callings. In particular he touches on poverty, chastity and obedience and their place in society today. There is here an unstated challenge to religious life – if the evangelical counsels are at the heart of religious life, how can they be made relevant, or, more importantly, how can their relevance be translated into something the world can see and understand? Specifically, how can religious show that obedience is not an abdication of responsibility and that chastity is not a form of sexual repression?

Finally, Teresa McCormack turns to the field of education and the involvement of religious. She writes of the radically alternative vision of society that many religious espouse and which lies at the heart of the gospel. In particular she focuses on the role of religious in education and the transfer of many religious from one form of education to another, for example, from traditional posts in teaching to working with community and adult education.

She writes that 'the education system, albeit inadvertently, is one of the principal mechanisms by which inequalities are preserved from one generation to the next.' In support of her argument she cites various statistics about the relationship between poverty and lack of access to education. Implicit in this is a questioning of the role of religious in education that CORI has been addressing for some time. Her suggestions are worthy of serious debate.

All in all, this second half of this volume only begins to address the data contained in John Weafer's report. It is not an end in itself but the beginning of a process. The future involvement of religious in Irish society is an important question in the face of declining numbers. Even if there were no great change in numbers, the questions raised here are critical – what is the appropriate response for religious today in Irish society? Where are the greatest needs and how can they be best addressed with the resources to hand? What shape will the response of generous men and women to the call of the gospel take in the future?

This volume is offered as a stimulus to the debate. It is a statement of where religious life is today, and a vision for its future. It is respectfully dedicated to all Irish religious, past and present, men and women, who committed their lives in the service of the gospel.

For to this end we toil and strive, because we have our hope set on the living God, who is the Saviour of all (I Tim 10:4).

Notes

1. Stephenson, Nathan L. 'Long-term Dynamics of Giant Sequoia Populations: Implications for Managing a Pioneer Species', Paper presented at the Symposium on Giant Sequoias: Their Place in the Ecosystem and Society, June 23-25, 1992, Visalia, California.
2. Kilgore, Bruce, 'Fire's Role in a Sequoia Forest', *National Parks & Conservation Magazine,* 44, 277: (Oct. 1970), 16-22

Profile of
Religious in Ireland

2

Introduction and Background to the Survey

John Weafer

1.1 Introduction

This report presents the major findings of a research project undertaken on behalf of the Conference of Religious of Ireland (CORI).[1] The principal objective of the research was to produce accurate and up-to-date statistical information on religious personnel working and living in Ireland. In 1989, the then Conference of Major Religious Superiors commissioned a similar piece of research that was published under the title of *Profile of Religious in Ireland, 1989-1990.*[2] Ten years later, CORI considered it timely that the study should be replicated to monitor the many changes that have taken place in the demographics and ministries of Irish religious in the interim. The principal aim of both surveys was to assist the Conference and the individual congregational leaders plan for an uncertain future by facilitating an informed response to the needs of religious congregations at this time.[3]

Within the parameters set by this core objective, the research also gathered statistical and other relevant information on the following areas:

- Total number of religious in Ireland.
- Age profile of religious personnel.
- Entrants, deaths and departures.
- Location of religious personnel.
- Community numbers and size.
- Number of religious personnel engaged in a wide variety of ministries.
- Qualifications and status of personnel in ministries.
- The views of congregational leaders on important trends impacting on religious life in Ireland.
- Concerns and hopes of congregational leaders for the future.

The study is set against a general context of declining vocations to most religious orders and congregations, an ageing and less active personnel, a movement away from institutional ministry to pastoral involvement, the growth of a more critical stance on religious and their contribution to Irish society,[4] and a certain lack of clarity concerning the role of religious in contemporary Ireland.[5] However, the context is also one of continuing service and dedication by substantial numbers of religious in the fields of education, health, pastoral ministries, social services and other ministries. Since different commentators tend to emphasise one aspect of religious life over another, it is important to document the reality in an objective and comprehensive manner. Accordingly, the present study seeks to describe the statistical reality of Irish religious in an accurate and comprehensive manner.

1.2 Research Approach

Each of the 127 congregations listed in CORI's *Address Guide 2000* received a self-completion postal questionnaire in November 1999. The questionnaire was addressed to the congregational leader and comprised two main sections: a demographic profile of the congregation and a section that sought the views of these leaders on various aspects of religious life in Ireland. Allowing for some changes to its format and content, the questionnaire replicated that sent in the earlier 1989 study. The final reply was received in May 2000, following three written reminders, e-mails, and numerous telephone and personal contacts. Overall, a response rate of 92% was achieved. In the case of the eleven congregations that did not reply, nine were female and most have a nominal presence in Ireland at the present time. An estimate for the non-responding congregations is included in the profile of religious presented in this report.

This study is essentially an independent piece of research and direct comparisons with previous surveys should be made with some caution. The *Profile of Religious in Ireland, 1989-1990* is the closest of the previous surveys conducted since 1971. The questionnaires used in both the 1989 and 1999 surveys were very similar and the universe of congregations included was also very similar. However, there are some differences that should be borne in mind when making comparisons between both surveys. Firstly, the 1989 study included a number of secular institutes, while the present survey was confined to personnel in religious congregations.[6] Secondly, it is possible that the geographical/administrative areas of some congregations have changed in the past ten years, with some congregations expanding their area of responsibility and others contracting. Thirdly, it is clear from the comments of many congregational leaders that demographic information on religious personnel is maintained in a variety of ways and that the format of these records has changed for some congregations over the years. Fourthly, while the present survey includes all personnel attached to Irish congregations, the 1989 survey would appear to have been limited to Irish personnel living and/or working in Ireland at the time of the research. The 1999 research adopted the broader approach of the earlier 1971 and 1981 surveys.[7]

Accordingly, although comparisons are made with the 1989 survey, the results from the present research should be treated as an independent piece of research in the first instance. Comparisons with the 1989 survey are most useful in pointing to overall trends that have occurred over the past ten years.

References

Conference of Major Religious Superiors, 1990, *Profile of Religious in Ireland 1989-1990* Dublin: CMRS.

Nygren, D. and Ukeritis, M., 1993, *The Future of Religious Orders in the United States: Transformation and Commitment* Westport: Praeger.

Weafer, J. and Breslin, A. 1983, *Irish Catholic Clergy and Religious 1970-1981* Maynooth: Council for Research and Development.

Weafer, J. 2000, 'Irish Attitudes Towards Religious: A National Survey' in *Religious Life Review* Vol. 39, No. 203.

Notes

1. The information requested from the congregations related to personnel attached to the Irish congregation (province/region), regardless of their present location. In this and previous surveys, the term Ireland refers to the island of Ireland.
2. The Council for Research and Development (Maynooth) conducted the first major study of Irish diocesan clergy and religious order personnel in 1971. The Council carried out a second study in 1981 to highlight any significant changes that had taken place within diocesan clergy and religious orders in the intervening ten years (Weafer and Breslin, 1983). The 1989 research focused almost exclusively on religious congregations and excluded diocesan clergy (CMRS, 1990).
3. In the introductory letter that accompanied the despatch of questionnaires to congregational leaders, the secretary general of CORI, Sr Elizabeth Maxwell, put the research in context: *'The issues which gave rise to the need* [for the 1989 survey] *were listed as those of forward planning, identification of trends which might*

facilitate change and a call for a response in our Church and our world, and the call for collaboration among religious. Ten years later it seems highly desirable that a somewhat similar survey be conducted. Changes have taken place in the demographics of Religious in Ireland. There has been a significant move from institutional ministry to pastoral involvement and the climate in Ireland in which religious work has altered dramatically.'

4. For further information on the views of Irish people towards religious in Ireland, see Weafer (2000). This study reports the views of a recent national study of 1,400 Irish adults towards religious in Ireland.
5. The current trend of change and decline in the demographics of religious orders is not unique to Ireland. Nygren and Ukeritis, for instance, observed similar trends in their study of more than 121,000 sisters, brothers and religious priests in the United States: *'The study emerges at a time when the average age of the members of many congregations in the United States approaches 67 years of age for women and 60 years of age for men while, over the period ranging from 1962 to 1992, the number of members of Roman Catholic religious orders has decreased by nearly 43% for brothers and sisters and 18% for religious priests. This decline corresponds with a comparable decline in Roman Catholic health, education and social service institutions'* (1993: xix).
6. In the case of the 1989 study, a total of 207 questionnaires were distributed by post to each Major Superior with members resident in Ireland. This number included both members and non-members of the Conference. While this number is significantly higher than the 127 questionnaires despatched in the case of the present survey, the difference is not as substantial as might initially appear since a number of congregations have amalgamated into national and/or regional congregations in the intervening ten years. The principal difference lies in the exclusion of non-conference members, specifically non-religious congregations, in 1999.
7. Unfortunately, the limited information still existing on the 1989 survey does not address this classification question. The instructions provided with the 1981 survey explicitly include members of an Irish Province who *'are working or studying abroad but are* ***not*** *members of another Province'*. This instruction was also applied in the present research.

3

Statistical Profile of Religious Personnel in Ireland

John Weafer

2.1 Total Religious Personnel

In November 1999, there were approximately 10,975 religious working and/or living in Ireland[1], compared with 15,634 in 1989 and 17,373 in 1981. When the number of Irish religious attached to Irish congregations working abroad is taken into account, the total number of Irish religious rises to 13,393.

Total Number of Religious in Ireland

	1999	1989*	1981*
Sisters	8,458	11,415	12,332
Brothers	735	1,178	1,490
Clerics	1,782	3,041	3,551
Total	10,975	15,634	17,373

(*Figures are not directly comparable from 1981 to 1999)

The corresponding figure for 1981 was 23,308. The majority (77%) of religious in Ireland are sisters, followed by clerical religious (16%) and brothers (7%).

When these results are compared directly with those from the previous 1989 and 1981 surveys, it would appear as if the number of Irish religious (including those based abroad) has declined by approximately 4,659 (-30%) since 1989 and 6,398 (-37%) since 1981. However, the actual decrease is likely to be substantially less than this figure when differences between the studies are taken into account. Specifically, the present research focused exclusively on religious congregations and excluded a number of secular congregations that had been included in previous surveys.[2] Other research collected in the course of this research suggests that the total decrease may be closer to 3,000 when the number of deaths, departures and entrants are taken into account. In the ten-year period covered by this research (1990–1999), 2,926 deaths occurred amongst Irish religious personnel. Furthermore, the number of people leaving religious congregations during this time (981) exceeded the total number of entrants (867). These figures suggest that the total decrease in numbers of religious personnel is closer to 3,000 than the 4,659 suggested earlier.

Entrants, Departures and Deaths, 1990-1999

	Entrants	Departures	Deaths	Balance (Entrants-Deaths, Departures)
Sisters	238	364	2,067	-2,193
Brothers	61	183	268	-390
Clerics	568	434	591	-457
Total	**867**	**981**	**2,926**	**-3,040**

The single largest decrease over the ten-year period is due to the death of religious. This figure was relatively consistent from year to year, with approximately 300 deaths recorded each year. The number of entrants and departures more or less balanced each other out over the ten-year period under review, with approximately 100 entering and departing each year. Approximately 400 of the 981 departures were by religious who had made final profession, followed by 216 'after first profession', 203 postulants and 161 novices.

2.2 Postulants, Novices and Professed Members

The majority of the 13,393 Irish religious are professed, with just 302 members who are postulants, novices or scholastics. Furthermore, as the following table indicates, most of the unprofessed members are based outside Ireland.

Table 1 Postulants, Novices and Professed Members, 1999

Category	Ireland	Outside Ireland	Total
Postulants	15	78	93
Novices	19	50	69
Scholastics	39	101	140
Professed Sisters	8,446	1,322	9,768
Professed Brothers	994	226	1,220
Priests	1,462	641	2,103
Total	**10,975**	**2,418**	**13,393**

Further analysis indicates that the majority of the 302 unprofessed members attached to Irish congregations belong to a relatively small number of clerical religious congregations. Although the information in the questionnaires does not differentiate religious by nationality, subsequent contact with a number of these congregations confirmed that many of these younger unprofessed personnel are indigenous to the country or region in which they are currently based and are unlikely to be of direct service to the Irish Church in the foreseeable future.

The information presented in Table 1 above also confirms the strong 'missionary' dimension of Irish congregations with 2,418 religious currently living and working abroad. Furthermore, many of this group are some of the younger religious in Ireland (see section 2.3, following).

2.3 Age Profile of Irish Religious[3]

Just over two thirds of Irish religious are aged 60 years of age or over, compared with only 11% who are less than 50 years of age. This overall trend is most acute for sisters' congregations where more than seven in ten sisters are 60 years of age or over and seven per cent are less than 50 years of age. Conversely, as the following chart illustrates, clerical religious congregations have a younger age profile than sisters' or brothers' congregations, with almost three in ten (28%) members under the age of 50.

Age Profile of Religious in Ireland, 1999

Age bands	Total %	Sisters %	Brothers %	Clerics %
Under 29 years	2.0	0.6	2.7	7.1
30-39 years	3.2	1.6	2.3	9.7
40-49 years	6.0	4.6	6.2	11.1
50-59 years	21.4	21.1	25.8	20.8
60-69 years	25.3	25.00	26.9	26.00
70-79 years	24.9	27.1	24.2	17.0
80+ years	17.2	20.0	12.0	8.3
Total	**100%**	**9,809 (100%)**	**923 (100%)**	**2,661 (100%)**

The location of the younger members is quite significant, with the majority (78%) of the youngest members (under 29 years) located outside Ireland.

Irish Religious by Age and Location, 1999

Age bands	Ireland Number	Abroad Number	Total Number	%
Under 29 years	59	214	273	2.0
30-39 years	253	180	433	3.2
40-49 years	606	202	808	6.0
50-59 years	2,263	597	2,860	21.4
60-69 years	2,768	623	3,391	25.3
70-79 years	2,950	386	3,336	24.9
80+ years	2,076	216	2,292	17.2
Total	**10,975**	**2,418**	**13,393**	**100**

The distribution of religious personnel by sector, age and location is presented in Table 2 below. In each case, the number of young religious abroad outnumbers those at home, whereas the opposite trend is apparent for the older religious. In total, there are 312 religious working in Ireland under 40 years of age. The corresponding figure for religious abroad is 394.

Table 2
Age Profile and Location of Irish Religious Personnel, 1999

Age Bands	Sisters (Number)		Brothers (Number)		Clerics (Number)		Total
	Ireland	Abroad	Ireland	Abroad	Ireland	Abroad	Total
Under 29	13	45	3	22	43	147	273
30-39	107	47	13	8	133	125	433
40-49	374	76	48	9	179	117	808
50-59	1,728	340	171	67	364	190	2,860
60-69	2,061	389	213	35	494	196	3,391
70-79	2,389	271	187	36	374	79	3,336
80+	1,785	184	100	11	196	24	2,292
Total	**8,457**	**1,352**	**735**	**188**	**1,783**	**878**	**13,393**

The overall demographic trends outlined above are in sharp contrast with the age profile of the Irish population. Approximately, 17% of the Irish Republic's adult population (20+ years) are 65 years of age or over, compared with just over half (54%) of Irish religious.

The gradual ageing of Irish religious is very apparent if the data from the present survey is compared with the 1989 results. In 1989, approximately one in ten religious were aged 80 years of age or over, compared with 17% of religious in 1999. Conversely, while 25% of religious in 1989 were aged less than 50 years of age, this figure had fallen to 11% in 1999.

Age Profile Comparison, 1989-1999

Age Bands	<29 %	30-39 %	40-49 %	50-59 %	60-69 %	70-79 %	80+ %
Sisters							
1999	**0.6**	**1.6**	**4.6**	**21.1**	**25.0**	**27.1**	**20.0**
1989*	2.0	4.8	16.0	20.2	23.2	22.2	11.6
Brothers							
1999	**2.7**	**2.3**	**6.2**	**25.8**	**26.9**	**24.2**	**12.0**
1989	5.2	7.6	19.0	21.3	20.8	19.9	6.2
Clerics							
1999	**7.1**	**9.7**	**11.1**	**20.8**	**26.0**	**17.0**	**8.3**
1989	8.8	8.0	14.5	28.1	19.6	16.8	4.2
Total							
1999	**2.0**	**3.2**	**6.0**	**21.4**	**25.3**	**24.9**	**17.2**
1989	3.6	5.6	16	21.8	22.3	21	9.7

* 1989 and 1999 figures not directly comparable.

2.4 Location of Irish Religious

Most Irish religious are working and/or living in Ireland, with approximately one in five religious based outside Ireland. The largest grouping of overseas personnel are based in Africa (n=920), followed by Britain (n=713), South/Central America (n=223), USA/Canada (n=209), Western Europe excluding Ireland and Britain (n=155), Asia (n=107), Australia/New Zealand (n=63), Eastern Europe (n=23) and India (n=5).

Location of Irish Religious, 1999

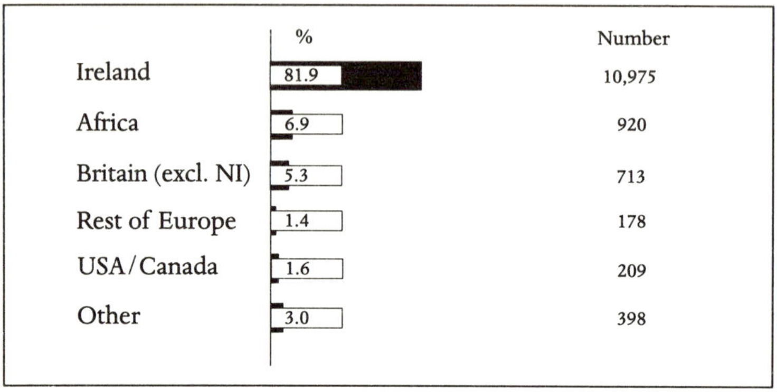

Location of Irish Religious by Sector, 1999

	In Ireland	Abroad	Total
Sisters	8,458	1,351	9,809
Brothers	735	188	923
Clerics	1,782	879	2,661
Total	**10,975 (82%)**	**2,418 (18%)**	**13,393 (100%)**

In the case of the 10,975 religious living and working in Ireland, the majority are based in Leinster (52%), followed by Munster (26%), Connacht (10%) and Ulster (11%). Allowing for different census periods in Northern Ireland and the Republic of Ireland, the total population of Ireland is distributed as follows: Leinster (37%), Munster (20%), Ulster (34%) and Connacht (8%). Accordingly, Leinster is over-represented by religious in absolute terms, while Ulster is under-represented. Further analysis indicates that just over half of the total population of religious is located in four counties: Dublin, Cork, Galway and Limerick.

Top Ten Counties – Number of Religious, 1999

	Number	% of Total (N=10,975)
Dublin	3,653	33.3
Cork	1,123	10.2
Galway	592	5.4
Limerick	546	5.0
Tipperary	398	3.6
Antrim	368	3.3
Waterford	352	3.2
Louth	342	3.1
Kildare	316	2.9
Kerry	317	2.9
Total	**8,007**	**72.9**

The active members of these congregations are fairly evenly distributed throughout the four Provinces, as the results in Table 3 illustrate. For instance, while half of all religious are based in Leinster, a similar proportion engaged in a fulltime ministry are also located in Leinster. The majority of all religious are located in Dublin.

Table 3 Location of Religious in Ireland by Full-time Ministry, 1999

Province	Total Religious in Ireland		Fulltime Ministry		
	Number	%	Sisters	Brothers	Clerics
Leinster	5,766	52.5	50.6	61.2	59.0
Munster	2,893	26.3	25.5	24.3	23.0
Connacht	1,144	10.4	13.7	8.6	6.8
Ulster	1,172	10.7	10.2	5.9	11.3
Total	**10,975**	**100%**	**100%**	**100%**	**100%**

Community Size by Religious Category, 1999

	Total		Sisters		Brothers		Clerics	
	Number	%	Number	%	Number	%	Number	%
Live Alone	624	4.7	348	3.5	19	2.1	257	9.7
2-5	3,970	29.6	2,755	28.1	395	42.8	820	30.8
6-10	3,144	23.5	2,211	22.5	326	35.3	607	22.8
11-20	3,202	23.9	2,564	26.1	158	17.1	480	18.0
21+	2,453	18.3	1,931	19.7	25	2.7	497	18.7
Total	**13,393**	**100**	**9,809**	**100**	**923**	**100**	**2,661**	**100**

2.5 Community Number and Size

Just over 600 religious live alone, while almost 2,500 religious live in communities of 21 or more members. Some differences emerged between the different religious categories in terms of their living arrangements: brothers are least likely to live alone and tend to be concentrated in communities of 2–10 members; sisters are more evenly spread across the different community sizes; while clerical religious have the highest proportion of members living alone. Many of this latter group are working in mission areas abroad.

Community Size, 1999

	In Ireland	Abroad	Total
Live alone	385 (3.5%)	239 (9.9%)	624 (4.7%)
2-5	2,718 (24.8%)	1,252 (51.8%)	3,970 (29.6%)
6-10	2,553 (23.3%)	591 (24.4%)	3,144 (23.5%)
11-20	3,027 (27.6%)	175 (7.2%)	3,202 (23.9%)
21+	2,292 (20.9%)	161 (6.7%)	2,453 (18.3%)
Total	**10,975 (100%)**	**2,418 (100%)**	**13,393 (100%)**

Q. Please indicate how many members live in the following community sizes?

Irish personnel living abroad are much more likely to live alone or in small communities when compared with their counterparts in Ireland where almost half (48.5%) live in communities of more than 10 people. Many of the clerics who are living alone outside of Ireland are engaged in parish ministry.

The total number of religious communities in Ireland has increased substantially over the past three decades, from 1,136 in 1970 to 1,838 in 1999. As the following chart indicates, most of this increase in the number of communities has occurred in the past ten years. In general, the number of sisters' communities has increased most, while the number of brothers' communities has decreased most.

Total Number of Religious Communities in Ireland, 1970-1999

	1999	1989	1981	1970
Sisters	1,335	1,022	850	723
Brothers	158	178	206	231
Clerics	345	241	224	182
Total	**1,838**	**1,450**	**1,280**	**1,136**

The trend in the number of religious communities noted above is also reflected in the number of communities that have opened and closed in the past five years. Overall, religious congregations have opened 289 community houses and closed 139 houses, resulting in 150 fewer community houses than was the case five years ago. Sisters' congregations have opened most community houses (n=221) during this period, followed by clerical religious (n=58) and brothers (n=10). Sisters' congregations have also closed the largest number of community houses over the past five years (n=92), followed by brothers (n=27) and clerical religious (n=20). These figures bear out the general trend for sisters to move from larger to smaller communities and for brothers to close communities altogether in specific areas.

Opening and Closing of Community Houses, 1999

Community Houses	Sisters	Brothers	Clerics	Total
Opened	221	10	58	289
Closed	92	27	20	139
Balance	**129**	**-17**	**38**	**150**

Q. How many community houses have opened/closed in the last five years?

2.6 Religious Ministries[4]

The second major section of the survey focused on the various ministries in which Irish religious are currently engaged. Each person was designated as having one 'fulltime' ministry if there were engaged in some form of active ministry. Religious who are more or less permanently sick or retired were classified as such. Individuals involved in a number of ministries were included as often as was appropriate under the heading of 'part-time' ministry[5] but only once under fulltime ministry. The information on ministries was recorded under the following nine headings[6]:

- Education
- Health Care
- Social Services
- Pastoral Services
- Justice
- Formation of Religious
- Community ministry
- Alternative ministries
- Other (retired, student)

The focus of this section is on the ministries rather than the individuals involved in the ministries. Accordingly, while information was provided on the total number of people involved in any one ministry, the personal characteristics of the individuals involved were not recorded or, in many cases, available in any systematic format. Such a study would have demanded considerably more time and resources than were available for the present study[7].

2.7 Overall Trends in Ministry

The results presented below and described in more detail in the pages following highlight a number of key trends in contemporary religious life: a substantial reduction in the number and proportion of religious working in the more traditional ministries of education and health care; a definite

Total Ministries, 1989-1999

	Total In Ministry 1999	Full-time 1999	Full-time 1989
Education	2,188	1,669 (12.4%)	4,091 (26.2%)
Health Care	972	809 (6.0%)	1,485 (9.5%)
Social Services	645	443 (3.3%)	89 (0.6%)
Pastoral Ministries	2,204	1,687 (12.5%)	1,337 (8.6%)
Justice	276	147 (1.1%)	162 (1.0%)
Formation of Religious	559	201 (1.5%)	518 (3.3%)
Community Ministry	2,367	1,471 (11.0%)	1,915 (12.2%)
Alternative Ministries	89	48 (0.4%)	Not available
Retired	6,314	6,314 (47.1%)	
Student	307	307 (2.3%)	
Leave/Sabbatical	297	297 (2.2%)	
Total		**13,393 (100%)**	

* 1989 and 1999 figures not directly comparable.

movement towards pastoral and social ministries; the substantial proportion of religious who are classified as 'fulltime' retired/sick; and the large number of religious who are engaged in a variety of ministries on a regular basis.

Approximately half of all Irish religious (n=6,475) are currently actively engaged in a fulltime ministry, with most of the remainder (n=6,314) falling into the fully retired/sick category. However, as the figures in the chart above clearly illustrate, the contribution of Irish religious exceeds that of 6,475 individuals, since a substantial proportion of these 'active' religious also work in other ministries in a part-time capacity.

2.8 Education Ministry

Almost 1,700 Irish religious are engaged in the education ministry on a fulltime basis, with a further 519 religious who work in this ministry part-time. The vast majority of these religious are qualified for their work, particularly where they are engaged in a formal school setting. Despite the substantial decrease in the number of religious working in this ministry since 1989, the involvement of religious in education is nevertheless considerable, with more than 1,200 religious working fulltime in primary and second level schools. Apart from the total reduction in the number of religious employed in the education ministry, the principal change in the statistical profile of this ministry is the movement away from the formal school setting to community, adult and third-level education. Three quarters of the religious who work fulltime in the education ministry are female.

The 'other' ministries that individual congregations felt could not be incorporated into the given categories included: media (8), home school liaison (7), art (5), religious education/catechetics (5), remedial/resource teacher (4), writing (3), language school (3), education of homeless (3), diocesan advisor music teacher (2), education officer, drama, school helper, secretary, special needs, holistic education, economics, conference centre, and library.

Education Ministry, 1989-1999

	Total Full-time, 1999				Total Full-time
	Sisters	Brothers	Clerics	Total '99	1989
Pre-School	20	-	-	20	46
Primary Teacher	392	34	1	427	1,202
Principal	246	45	16	307	727
Second Level Teacher	387	102	39	528	1,711
Teacher training	8	10	1	19	34
Third Level	20	4	61	85	41
Adult Education	47	13	6	66	59
Career Guidance Counselling	22	1	2	25	69
Special Schools	23	13	3	39	78
Administration In Educational Institutions	34	13	17	64	124
Community education	25	7	-	32	n/a
Other	35	8	14	57	n/a
Total Education	**1,259**	**250**	**160**	**1,669**	**4,091**

2.9 Health Care Ministry

The provision of health care continues to occupy the time and energy of substantial number of Irish religious, with more than 800 religious engaged fulltime and a further 163 members working part-time in this ministry. Once again, the vast majority of religious working fulltime in this ministry have an appropriate professional qualification for the work in which they are engaged. A movement from traditional, institutional medical care to more pastoral health care is evident from the following chart, with many religious working in the community, with HIV patients, and in pastoral situations, generally. More than nine in ten religious who work fulltime in this ministry are female.

Health Care Ministry

	Total Full-time, 1999				Total Full-time 1989
	Sisters	Brothers	Clerics	Total '99	
Doctor/Specialist	8	-	1	9	35
Health Care – Administration	134	14	1	149	152
General Nursing	216	2	1	218	661
Geriatric Nursing	127	-	-	132	92
Psychiatric Nursing	3	3	-	6	21
Mentally Handicapped	21	11		32	88
Addiction Centres	20	3	1	24	13
Physically Handicapped	11	-	-	11	10
Community Nursing	67	-	-	67	63
Nurse Tutor	9	-	-	9	28
Working with HIV Patients	31	1	3	35	n/a
Other	106	1	14	117	322
Total Health Care	**753**	**35**	**21**	**809**	**1,485**

The 'other' health care ministries included: carers (36), pastoral (23), hospice (11), rural African clinics (10), hospital chaplain (8), nursery home (2), care of elderly parents (2), domestic/reception (2), school infirmary (2), prison nurse, physiotherapy, laboratory technician, pharmacist, and behaviour change programme.

2.10 Social Services Ministry

The ministry of social services has experienced considerable growth over the past ten years, with approximately five times the number of religious engaged in a fulltime capacity in 1999 than was the case in 1989. Just over three in ten (n=202) religious who work in this ministry do so on a part-time basis. Once again, the majority of religious working fulltime in this ministry are female. Most of the 443 religious who work on a fulltime capacity in this ministry have an 'appropriate' professional qualification. The number of religious who are working fulltime in this ministry but who are considered by their congregational leaders *not* to have an 'appropriate' professional qualification are spread across the following areas of work: community work (12), social work (5), youth work (10), residential homes (15), hostels (17) and 'other' (8).

Social Services Ministry, 1989-1999

	Total Full-time, 1999				Total Full-time
	Sisters	**Brothers**	**Clerics**	**Total '99**	**1989**
Comunity Work	96	6	7	109	8
Social Work	56	5	1	63	51
Youth Work	34	2	6	44	6
Residential Homes	36	-	5	41	n/a
Special Schools	8	-	-	8	8
Hostels	25	1	2	28	16
Child guidance	3	-	-	3	n/a
Counselling	106	3	11	120	n/a
Other	27	3	-	27	n/a
Total Social Services	**391**	**20**	**32**	**443**	**89**

The 'other' social services ministries included: day-care centre (7), family ministry (5), outreach to elderly (2), work with alcoholics, parish social work, psychologist, warden – senior citizen, riding for disabled, and CORI.

2.11 Pastoral Services Ministry

The number of religious engaged fulltime in pastoral services ministries has also increased over the past ten years, particularly in the areas of pastoral work and chaplaincy and in the role of parish priest. The number of religious engaged fulltime in retreat work has remained more or less consistent in the intervening ten-year period. While the majority of religious working fulltime in this ministry have an appropriate professional qualification, a substantial number do not: pastoral workers/parish ministry (232), hospital chaplain (27), prison chaplain (11), school chaplain (17), youth chaplain (1), retreats (36), and 'other' (22). In addition to the 1,687 religious who work fulltime in this ministry, a further 517 members are involved in a part-time capacity.

Pastoral Services Ministry, 1989-1999

	Total Full-time, 1999				Total Full-time
	Sisters	Brothers	Clerics	Total '99	1989
Curates	-	-	236	236	253
Parish Priests	-	2	192	194	65
Priests Ministering in Churches	-	-	391	391	319
Pastoral Workers/Parish Ministry	409	7	19	435	286
Chaplaincy – Hospital	57	3	40	100	70
Chaplaincy – Prisons	22	2	6	30	5
Chaplaincy – Education	44	-	32	76	61
Chaplaincy – Youth	7	-	6	13	24
Retreats	58	5	87	150	163
Other	30	-	32	62	91
Total Pastoral Ministry	**627**	**19**	**1,041**	**1,687**	**1,337**

Note: *Two individuals in a brother's order are priests.*

The 'other' pastoral services ministries included: pastoral care of elderly (31), counselling (4), missionary animation (3), hermitage (3), spiritual direction (2), religious advisor (2), army chaplain (2), prison ministry, marriage tribunal, bishop, parish secretary, clinical pastoral education, pioneer PTA, residential chaplain, garda chaplain, diocesan pastoral development, prayer ministry and ministry to retired priests.

2.12 Justice Ministry

The total number of religious recorded as working fulltime in the justice ministry has dropped slightly since 1989, from 162 to 147, with an additional 129 religious working in a part-time capacity. Within this total figure, there was considerable movement away from a focus on disadvantaged areas to centres of faith and justice. The area of Travellers was identified as a separate category of the justice ministry in 1999. Just over half of the people who work fulltime in this ministry have an appropriate professional qualification. The areas in which qualifications are lacking are: emigrants (6), homeless (12), disadvantaged areas (11), centres for faith and justice (16), Travellers (14), research/policy-making (1), unemployed (2) and 'other' (1).

Justice Ministry, 1989-1999

	Total Full-time, 1999				Total Full-time
	Sisters	Brothers	Clerics	Total '99	1989
Emigrants	9	1	3	13	16
Homeless	28	1	2	31	35
Unemployed	2	-	-	2	9
Disadvantaged Areas	42	1	-	43	76
Centres for Faith and Justice	25	-	4	29	8
Research/Policy Making	2	-	3	5	6
Travellers	15	1	2	18	n/a
Other	2	1	3	6	12
Total Justice	**125**	**5**	**17**	**147**	**162**

2.13 Formation Ministry

Approximately, 200 religious continue to be engaged in a fulltime capacity in the general area of religious formation, representing a significant reduction on the 1989 number, although when the number of religious involved in a part-time capacity is included (n=358), the total number of religious who are active in this ministry exceeds 550. The change is most noticeable in the areas of 'philosophical/theological institutes', seminaries, formation courses, and on-going formation. The areas in which fulltime workers do not have appropriate fulltime qualifications are: pre-novitiate (4), junior professed (5), on-going formation (5), vocation awareness (19), seminaries (2), philosophical/ theological institutes (2) and 'other'. The category 'novitiate' was inadvertently excluded from the questionnaire. Accordingly, it is assumed that most of the 'other' category refers to this category of formation.

Formation of Religious, 1989-1999

	Total Full-time, 1999				Total Full-time
	Sisters	Brothers	Clerics	Total '99	1989
Pre-Novitiate	14	5	13	32	40
Junior Professed	12	3	20	35	45
On-going Formation	11	1	10	22	43
Vocation Awareness	19	5	10	34	84
Seminaries	5	2	13	20	46
Courses For Formation	10	5	3	18	38
Philosophical/Theological Institutes	4	1	18	23	94
Other	8	2	7	17	12
Total Formation	**83**	**24**	**94**	**201**	**402**

2.14 Community Ministry

Community ministry accounts for the fulltime ministry of almost 1,500 religious, with an additional 896 who work in a part-time capacity. Most of these religious are engaged in leadership positions, house ministry, or administration on behalf of the congregation. Overall, the number of religious working fulltime in this ministry has declined by approximately one quarter since 1989. The number of leaders who believe

Community Ministry, 1999

	Total in Ministry	Total Full-time	Total Qualified
	Number	Number	Number
Congregational/Provincial/ Regional/Leadership	376	256	109
Business/Financial/ Congregational Administration	250	163	86
Archives/Research	83	49	29
Promotion/Fundraising	115	62	6
House Ministry	914	493	98
Farming/Gardening	46	21	8
Infirmary	134	70	39
Working with other Churches	18	8	2
Local Leadership	136	122	-
Monastic Life	197	197	197
Other	98	30	25
Total Community Ministry	**2,367**	**1,471**	**599**

they do not have an 'appropriate professional' qualification for their role as lead or administrator is indicative perhaps, of the non-specific nature of these positions.

The 'other' category included: community churches (44), secretarial (8), media (3), sacristan (3), secretary to bishop (2), ministry development (2), ecological farming (2), CORI, student hostel, and community chaplain.

2.15 Alternative Ministries

The 1999 survey included a new section on alternative ministries, covering areas such as aromatherapy, healing and any other area the individual congregation deemed appropriate to include in this general category. In total, 48 religious are working fulltime in this area, with a similar number engaged in a part-time capacity. Most (33) have an appropriate professional qualification for their work.

Notes

1. Unless otherwise stated, all references to Ireland in this study refer to the 32 counties of Ireland.
2. The CMRS 1989 research included 23 non-conference members, many of which have relatively large memberships (e.g. Society of African Missions, Missionaries for Africa, Columban Fathers, Mill Hill Fathers, St. Patrick's Missionary Society, etc.). These were excluded from the 1999 research.
3. Unless otherwise stated, the data summarised in this chapter refers to the total number of Irish religious, regardless of their present location.
4. This section is based on the 13,393 religious attached to Irish congregations, regardless of their present location. Due to the differences in the research design used in both studies, comparisons with the 1989 research should be regarded as indicative rather than absolute.
5. This section was, perhaps, the most difficult of all for congregational leaders to complete for a number of reasons. Firstly, it would appear that few congregations keep this type of information on individual religious in any systematic or comprehensive way, particularly in relation to the many part-time ministries in which their members are involved. Secondly, quite a number of religious are engaged in a variety of ministries and it was often difficult for congregational leaders to decide which of the ministries is their main 'fulltime' ministry. Thirdly, there would appear to be a degree of freedom accorded to religious who have reached 'retirement' age, with the result that their specific activities are not always known by their leaders at congregational level.
6. With one exception, alternative ministries, similar categories were used in the present survey as were used in the 1989 research. However, direct comparisons should be made with some caution in the case of those categories which are open to some interpretation. For instance, a person working within the context

of a parish may be included in one of a number of different but similar categories: justice, pastoral ministry, or even social services. While each category was broken down into individual ministries to assist the allocation of members into the most appropriate ministry, the ultimate decision was made by the congregational leader.

7. A sample survey of religious is the more standard way in which this type of information is collected. See, for example, the study of religious in the United States by D. Nygren and M. Ukeritis (1993), op. cit.

4

Trends in Religious Life

John Weafer

3. Introduction

This section of the survey was directed exclusively at congregational leaders and elicited their views on a number of issues relating to religious life in Ireland: the most important trends in religious life; their concerns and hopes for their congregation; and their general feelings towards religious life now and in the future.

3.1 Important Trends in Religious Life

The congregational leaders were given a list of fourteen trends in religious life and asked to indicate how important these trends were for their congregation at the present time. The list included the following:

- rediscovery of original purpose of the institute
- solidarity with the poor
- justice concerns
- cosmology
- greater collaboration with diocesan clergy

- greater collaboration with other religious
- greater collaboration with lay people
- experimenting with new expressions of religious and community life
- openness to new forms of religious and community life
- oppression of your members as a result of membership in your congregation
- experimenting with new forms of prayer
- openness to new forms of prayer
- identifying new needs
- influencing public policy

The areas that were considered most important for their congregations at this time were:

Most Important Trends in Religious Life

Base: All Respondents – Congregational Leaders (n=113)

1. Solidarity with the poor
2. Greater collaboration with lay people
3. Justice concerns
4. Rediscovery of original purpose of the institute
5. Openness to new forms of religious and community life
6. Greater collaboration with other religious.

Q. Which of these areas do you consider to be the most important for your Congregation at this time?

Conversely, the areas that were regarded as least important were: oppression of your members as a result of membership in your congregation, cosmology, influencing public policy, experimenting with new expressions of religious and community life, experimenting with new forms of prayer, and greater collaboration with diocesan clergy.

3.1 Concerns for Congregation

When asked to list any concerns they have for their congregation over the next five to ten years, the congregational leaders put most emphasis on: ageing members and diminishing personnel numbers, care of elderly members and maintaining present resources, making consecrated life more relevant to modern life, and lack of vocations.

Concerns for Congregation

Base: All Respondents – Congregational Leaders (n=113)

	Number of times mentioned	% of total (n=113)
• Ageing members; diminishing numbers; maintaining vitality of Congregation	44	39
• Maintaining present membership and resources; care of elderly; financial embarrassment	43	38
• Finding new ways of expressing commentment to charism; make consecrated life more relevant to modern world	43	38
• Lack of vocations; no new life coming through	37	33
• (Forced) Rationalisation of houses, schools, etc	14	12

Q. What concerns do you have for your Congregation over the next five to ten years?

Other concerns mentioned by these leaders included. rationalisation (forced) of houses, schools, etc. (n=14), not to get bogged down in the maintenance of the congregation with a consequent loss of vision for the congregation (n=17), and that they might become too secure in their present lifestyle and not be willing to take the necessary risks (n=16).

3.2 Hopes for Congregation

The principal hopes for their congregations included: remaining faithful to the charism in vibrant and creative ways, renewing the passion for religious life, greater collaboration with like-minded individuals and groups, an increase in vocations, providing real support for each other, and having the courage to find new forms of religious life.

Hopes for Congregation

Base: All Respondents – Congregational Leaders (n=113)

	Number of times mentioned	% of total (n=113)
• Remain faithful to charism; life it vibrantly and with creativity	34	30
• Renewal of passion and values of religious life	28	25
• Greater collaboration and networking with like-minded individuals and groups	26	23
• Continue to be inventive in our ministry; respond to real needs; identifying unmet needs	24	21
• Increase in vocations	21	19
• Live truly inclusive Christian community; support each other	21	19
• Courage and openness to new forms of religious life	21	19

Q. What hopes do you have for your Congregation over the next five to ten years?

3.3 Feelings Towards Religious Life

The majority (74%) of congregational leaders are either enthusiastic or hopeful towards religious life. Most of the remainder have somewhat mixed opinions and are 'sometimes hopeful/not hopeful' towards religious life. Their reasons for feeling this way are quite varied, as the following chart illustrates.

Future of Religious Life in Ireland

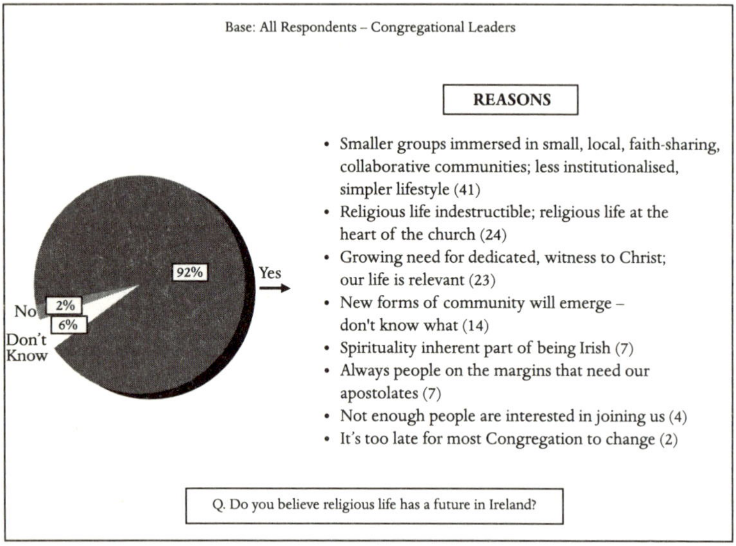

Finally, more than nine in ten leaders believe religious life has a future in Ireland, even if, for many of them, the future is different from its present form. Many leaders feel that religious life will survive in smaller groups that are immersed in local communities with a simpler and less institutionalised lifestyle.

Reflections

5

Apostolic Religious Life in Ireland and Western Europe

Elizabeth Maxwell PBVM

Inside religious orders and congregations and outside, particularly in the media world, there is a tendency to equate numbers with success. In the face of declining membership and the weak trickle of new candidates for the life today it is not unusual to hear religious in Ireland speak nostalgically of the good old days of the late 1950s and early 1960s when the number of vocations caused congregational leaders to initiate building programmes to house the new members. We now know that the leaders of that period failed to read the signals that change was coming. By 1967 the peak in membership had been reached. In the years that followed a steady decline was evident, affected undoubtedly by the climate of reflection and questioning that the experience of Vatican II made possible.

Decline: Result of Scandals?

There are media commentators in Ireland today who attribute the decline in numbers in religious life to the scandals and revelations in the 1990s of abusive behaviour on the part of some clergy and religious. No analysis could be more facile or untrue. In 1967 there were 29,984 religious in Ireland. In 1970 the first downturn in the numbers of applicants to religious life became evident. By 1999 the total number of religious in the country was 16,046. In 1967 the number of new applicants to religious life in Ireland totalled 1,018. In 1999 that number was 45.[1]

Religious as service providers

The phenomenal growth in membership of religious congregations experienced in Ireland in the late 1940s and throughout the 1950s and 1960s is frequently alluded to by writers but rarely explained, theologically or sociologically. That the dramatic increase in vocations is linked to cultural phenomena seems worthy of consideration when we note that in 1800 there were, according to Corish (1985)[2], 120 nuns in the country. By 1850 that number had multiplied more than ten-fold. By 1870 there were 3,700 on record and by 1900 there were 8,000. It seems reasonable to suggest that the social, political and ecclesial climate that prevailed post Catholic Emancipation in 1829 made the growth in membership of religious life possible. In addition to the steady rise in the numbers entering the indigenous Irish congregations in the nineteenth century a steady stream of religious orders and congregations from mainland Europe made foundations here. Drawing on the teaching and healing ministries of Jesus as inspiration, they, with the indigenous congregations, contributed significantly to the establishment of the education and healthcare systems, which the population of Ireland so badly needed.

With the establishment of Ireland's political independence early in the twentieth century, the political and ecclesial structures welcomed the mission of the active apostolic religious, seeing in them valuable service providers, on the one hand, and, on the other, valuable instruments in the process of evangelisation and faith development. Throughout the late

1920s and early 1930s of the twentieth century the Holy Spirit continued to inspire new expressions of religious life in Ireland as we see in the development of new congregations such as the Medical Missionaries of Mary, the Columban Sisters and the Holy Rosary Sisters whose primary task, like that of the missionary societies of St Patrick and St Columban, was mission 'ad gentes'. In this outreach they re-echoed the 'peregrinare pro Christo' of the Irish monks in earlier centuries.

Post Vatican II – a changed world

The decline, then, in numbers of candidates applying to active religious orders and congregations of men and women in Ireland has been steady since 1970. This decline is inevitably the result of internal as well as external factors. If we accept that the climate of reflection and renewal inspired by the documents of Vatican II brought about a reappraisal of the role of religious within the Christian faith community, and heightened an appreciation of the role of the laity within the same faith community, we may be identifying some of the 'internal' factors. That a similar drop in the number of people entering religious life in other countries of Western Europe took place suggests that the experience in Ireland was part of a larger whole shared by Christian communities in the western world and possibly influenced also by social, economic and cultural factors that were external to the world of the active religious. Among these factors one might include the trend towards the privatisation of religious belief and the rejection of the community dimension, the individualisation of personal life, the growing rejection of all forms of institutional authority daring to offer a moral viewpoint, rising consumerism in an increasingly affluent society and the loss of a sense of the transcendent.

Compared with other Western European countries, Ireland still has a significantly higher proportion of religious to the general population, one that is nearer to a 'normal' distribution than perhaps the peak figures of 1967 represented.

The following Table is based on figures supplied by UCESM[3] for 1999:

Country	Total Population (million)	% of General Population
Austria	8.1	0.112%
Belgium	10.25	0.190%
France	59.0	0.098%
Italy	57.0	0.205%
Portugal	10.0	0.091%
Spain	39.7	0.171%
UK/Wales	50.9	0.019%
Ireland	**3.7**	**0.38%**

While the emerging reality of the number of religious in Ireland may be approaching a norm shared across western European countries, and while there are still nearly 3,000 more religious women in the country than there was a hundred years ago[4], the rising age profile of the group gives rise to a new set of concerns for congregational leaders and membership in particular, around healthcare and provision for retirement for large numbers of people who are now aged 60+ and over. This has huge financial as well as ministry-related implications for the religious as they are forced to withdraw from areas of work in which they have been traditionally heavily invested.

Where there are religious in formation attached to Irish provinces of orders and congregations, they are, for the most part in developing countries. This is a matter for rejoicing in the Churches of the Third World and is a logical extension of the work of the Irish religious on the missions. However, the newly professed religious will not replace the ageing religious on the home mission in Ireland.

Is there life behind the statistics?

> *It is equilibrium, not change that is fatal.*[5]
> *Sandra Schneiders*

One of the more interesting statistics presented in this research is the increase in the number of religious communities in Ireland from 1,136 in 1989 to 1,838 in 1999. As G. Arbuckle (1986) notes, one of the 'major achievements' of Vatican II was to

> destabilise in order to renew a religious culture that had grown old and tired and could hardly comprehend, let alone cope with, the demands of a rapidly changing world.[6]

The transition out of the institutional style of living in large convents and monasteries of 20–40 people into smaller groupings of 3-5 people had profound effects on the style of community life led by religious. Synonymous with the larger institutional lifestyle was the practice of the 'common life' in which all members followed a set timetable of prayer, dining and recreation together. This was essentially a monastic style of life but was the norm of many institutes of active apostolic life following on the Code of Canon Law 1917, which equated 'common life' with 'community life'. Vatican II, in urging religious to rediscover the original founding intention of their founders and foundresses, set them on a path that revealed how inappropriate, in many instances, the monastic style was to their particular charism.

Many religious moved into housing estates in a desire to live among the people of God and to work towards their empowerment where such a need existed. The intention was laudable. The experience was often painful. The challenge to move from the dependence mode engendered in institutional living to a more interdependent way of living together came as a surprise to many. That religious have continued to work through these challenges internally, regardless of their age profile, is a matter for continued hope and points to their willingness to adapt to the changing circumstances occasioned by Vatican II's destabilisation effect. New forms of communal prayer have arisen and the inclusion of local people in the prayer life of religious communities is increasingly reported.

Another consequence of the movement away from the institution was the gradual adoption of contemporary dress and the consequent loss of the identifying 'habit', which was such a distinctive mark of many congregations. The loss of the habit, which, in many instances, had its origins in the modes of dress of earlier centuries, is a cause of nostalgic regret on the part of many good people, but it has also contributed hugely to the invisibility factor that affects religious today. John Weafer's survey among 1,400 Irish adults aged 15 and over indicates that 41% claim to have no contact with religious today.[7] Not alone are these people not in contact, but the loss of a visible sign of the existence and presence of religious, the habit, means that they are not reminded of their existence. In an age when the branding of products is such a high priority in our culture, and where a picture is acknowledged as the most powerful means of telling the story, this invisibility factor may be a cause for concern. On the other hand, this value of a high exposure, which the marketing world prizes, is at variance with the intentions of most founders and foundresses of religious institutes. Recently reviewing a biography of Jean Claude Colin, founder of the Marist Fathers, Dr Michael Kennedy quotes Colin's desire that his followers be 'unknown and practically hidden in this world'.[8] The same impulse to be a leaven in the mass – indistinguishable – is expressed by the members of secular institutes today. They live and work side by side with their colleagues in every walk of life without any distinctive sign of their life of consecration.

Related to the movement out of the institutional style of life is another development in lifestyle, that of religious living singly. The figures show that 624 religious live alone. Over a third of these are priests working in parish ministry. The growth in the number of female religious living on their own points to a willingness on their part to detach from the community for the sake of the ministry and, in some cases, to an acknowledgement that community living, can be, at times, so lacking in support that it is preferable to live apart. These developments in community living call for a redefinition of what has traditionally been understood as community life and a re-examination of the relationship between community living and mission. Increasingly, community living is defined as a union of hearts and minds sustained by the distinctive charism of the Institute and nourished by focussed gatherings of the members rather than simply physically living together under one roof. Obviously, living together in a group also calls for a union of hearts and minds, and a vocational bonding rather than a personal bonding, since members do not choose with whom they will live.[9]

A similar willingness to adapt is shown by the active religious congregations in relation to their ministry. The statistics indicate major shifts from institutional forms of ministry in education and healthcare to meet new and emerging needs of a pastoral nature. In the area of ministry, congregations are facing two important tasks. The first is the need to make responsible and prudent provision for the continuation of their charism, whether education or healthcare, into a future of which they may or may not continue to be a part. The second is to find a manner of responding to new and emerging needs for pastoral response in a way that does not entrap them alone in large institutions but rather affords them an opportunity to work collaboratively together as religious, and with other voluntary and statutory bodies, in responding to the cry of the poor. As Pope John Paul II has noted:

> The consecrated life may experience further changes in its historical forms, but there will be no change in the substances of a choice which finds expression in a radical gift of self for love of the Lord Jesus and, in him, of every member of the human family.[10]

In the transitional years since Vatican II, apostolic religious in Europe have experienced something of an exile. They have had to leave so much that was precious and familiar behind: God himself, at times, seems to be eclipsed. In the darkness they search more deeply for His designs, treading the path of renewal, reading the signs of the times and longing for the 'new creation'.

> *Remember not the former things, nor consider the things of old*
> *Behold, I am doing a new thing.*
> Isaiah 43:18-19

The interior renewal of each religious is called for if religious life, as a radical response to the invitation to live out the evangelical counsels, is to become a reality. Success will be measured by fidelity.

Emerging signs of new life are visible in a number of developments that are taking place. The statistics indicate that the majority of young religious are in developing countries. Ireland's religious continue her mission 'ad gentes', not solely by engaging in evangelisation processes, but also by the formation of native religious who, in turn, will witness to the love of God for the poor in their own country. The restoration of religious freedom in former communist countries has opened up opportunities for mission in Eastern Europe that have been responded to by a number of apostolic religious from Ireland. New forms of community living are emerging in which congregations, male and female, collaborate to serve the mission of Jesus. A new found confidence in inviting young men and women to consider the call to religious life as a viable option was evident last year when two vocation promotion bodies took a stand at the RDS 'Opportunities 2000' Jobs Fair. Their slogan was 'Multinationals with a Difference: 2000 Opportunities!'. This year they challenged the visitors to a similar job opportunities fair with a question 'Still haven't found what you are looking for?' Religious no longer invite school leavers to join their formation programmes. The preferred candidate for religious life is the more mature applicant, possibly in his or her late 20s or early 30s, who has carried responsibility, taken important decisions in life and has experienced a measure of personal independence.

At the level of ministry the religious continue to show a capacity to spearhead responses to unmet needs in Irish society. Evidence for this is in

- the number of addiction treatment centres, including the only teenage addiction centre in Europe, set up in advance of any Government response to the crisis in substance abuse.

- at least four social housing agencies, which were set up by religious to address the need by lower income groups for affordable housing before the 'housing crisis' was publicly acknowledged.

- the development around the country of ecological projects by different groups of religious, inviting people to a spirituality centred on the Cosmic Christ and reflecting the growing consciousness of the need to care for the planet.

- the use of former Houses of Formation to offer retreats and opportunities for spiritual renewal to lay people, religious and clerics throughout the year.[11] From Derry to Kerry, from Larne to Wexford and from Galway to Dublin, the religious have adapted their lives and their buildings to changed circumstances in a positive response to the deep need for spirituality in society today.

- the involvement of religious in ecumenical work and, particularly, in their efforts to address the issue of sectarianism in Irish society.

- the response of religious to the developing pluralist character of Irish society by the development of a variety of projects to meet the needs of refugee and asylum seekers. Tapping into their experience of other cultures across Europe and in other continents, they have applied their knowledge of languages and their appreciation of the history and traditions of these people arriving into the country to ease their integration and to equip them with literacy skills required for dignified participation in Irish society.

Some challenges presented by 'Profile of Religious in Ireland'

Leaders of religious orders and congregations will find that this profile of religious in Ireland contains a number of challenges, some of which are administrative, some of which call for long-term strategic planning in relation to mission and ministry, and some of which pertain to our understanding of the nature of religious life itself.

One of the tasks of leadership, it seems to me, is to animate an ageing membership to live within a drastically changed cultural climate in which religious are no longer revered as essentially 'holy' people. The revelations in the 1990s of abusive behaviour on the part of some religious and clergy contributed to a sense of initial shock and bewilderment, which lingers as a pervasive experience of low morale in good people who once enjoyed a position of high esteem in Irish society. Religious and clergy in general are not unique in their experience of having fallen out of popular favour. Politicians and members of the medical profession, to name but two groups, are also experiencing a hostility that was not evident ten years ago. The trap will be for religious to begin to see themselves as victims of an unsympathetic press or to equate the value of their lives by the measure of the applause afforded their efforts to lead Gospel lives. Leaders, then, must find ways to address the low morale among their members and help them to joyfully witness, in an alien culture, that God is good.

A possible corollary of the need to eschew victimhood is the desirability of training religious to use media as a tool for evangelisation and bringing the Good News of the Gospel to a media dependent culture. Religious must transcend their fear of media, must engage professionally with these powerful means of communication and so work towards an integration of faith and culture.

> Consecrated persons ... have a duty to learn the language of the media, in order to speak effectively of Christ to our contemporaries, interpreting their 'joys and hopes, their griefs and anxieties.[12]

The call to live out the evangelical counsels in a community setting is an area that today calls for courageous leadership within orders and congregations of apostolic life. Leadership will necessitate reflection and study on the historical evolution of what 'community life' essentially involves and a recognition that many of the features that were once deemed essential ingredients were, in fact, organisational decisions that facilitated an orderly or 'common' life in buildings that housed large groups of people. At another level they were the result of a social construct in which adult women had to be 'protected' and so convent doors closed at 5.00 pm, visitors left and all further egress was forbidden. Vatican II, as already noted, facilitated a movement out of the large institutions into smaller, more normal housing units designed for 3-5 people. As D. O'Murchú notes, small communities are

> more conducive to deeper dialogue, greater sharing of life and vision and the possibility of exploring in greater depth the search for community in today's world.[13]

If religious are to be a counter-cultural sign in today's world of fragmented relationships it is particularly in this area of community that they will have something significant to offer. Only by a shared dialogue between the members will that union of hearts and minds grow that is the essence of community. The crisis of community living will be avoided to the extent that leaders can support the process of moving from the dependency model of living engendered by the institution to the interdependence that small groups sharing faith, reflecting on mission, and collaborating in ministry, require if they are to function well. The alternative is for more and more individuals to opt for independent living. This is not to pass judgement on the religious who have opted to live singly and apart from houses of the institute. There are historical precedents to attest to this way of living the evangelical counsels and being in ministry as valid.[14] But where a significant or growing number of members seek to detach themselves from living within communities, the responsibility is on leadership, with the involvement of the membership, to define in a new way what membership of the religious institute entails and to seek ways and engage in processes that lead towards a new and accepted understanding of what a union of hearts and minds entails.

Conclusion

In the 35 years that have elapsed since Vatican II, profound changes have been experienced by active apostolic religious, internally in their living style, externally in their work domain.

While no master plan was created to enable leaders to manage the consequences of these changes, congregations of active apostolic religious in Ireland have responded creatively, on the whole, to the changed environment in which they live and work. Guided by the Holy Spirit, through prayer and reflection and observing the 'signs of the times', they have journeyed through the desert towards land as yet unseen but full of hope that there is a future for religious life. It is noteworthy that 92% of the leaders of the orders and congregations surveyed by John Weafer expressed a hope for the continuation of religious life in Ireland despite the current high age profile of the membership.

In this hope they are supported by Pope John Paul II:

> The present difficulties which a number of Institutes are encountering in some parts of the world must not lead to a questioning of the fact that the profession of the evangelical counsels is an *integral part of the Church's life* and a much needed incentive towards even greater fidelity to the Gospel...[15]

The question of whether Ireland needs religious any longer is unavoidable. If, by the question, one means do we need religious to do the things they always did like teach in schools, nurse in hospitals, organise meals-on-wheels, etc., the answer is no. Ireland has an excellent body of trained professionals to teach and nurse and a sufficiently buoyant economy to provide social services to the needy when it chooses to do so.

If by the question one means do we have any need in our society for a counter-cultural way of life that witnesses to the call of the Gospel to transcend greed, hedonism and a desire for domination, yes, Ireland still needs consecrated life in whatever shape or form it is destined to perdure.

Consecrated Life has been part of Ireland's history since the fifth century AD. It has contributed to our culture, our spirituality, our art and architecture, our literature and our music. Across Europe and every other continent, the contribution of Irish religious has built up and enriched communities. When Ireland recently won its place on the UN Security Council, both the Taoiseach and Brian Cowen, Minister for Foreign Affairs, listed the work of Irish missionaries as contributing to the positive image of Ireland among the voting member States.

The arena for the ministry of Irish religious today is not solely the island of Ireland with specific needs to be addressed, whether spiritual or temporal. Rather the arena is an increasingly globalised world in which Ireland contributes to decisions that affect the lives of millions of people abroad in other countries and on other continents.

Through their collaborative initiative in the establishment of the Conference of Religious of Ireland (CORI), religious in Ireland have created a vehicle by which, collectively, they can make their voice heard and influence public policy on behalf of the marginalised in Irish society. Through CORI's membership of the European Union of Conferences of Religious (UCESM) they have possibilities for extended influence at the level of the European Union and of the Council of Europe in shaping a future that is inclusive and which defends the rights of peoples of every race and creed. Tony Fahey (1998) speaking at the 10th anniversary of CORI's Social Policy Conference, observes that

> the new models of Catholic social actions which are now being created suggest that smaller numbers, concentrated and deployed at the cutting edge of social policy, can have an impact on the shape of future developments that matches, and may even exceed, anything achieved in the past.[16]

Thus, declining numbers of religious, by repositioning

themselves and redefining their roles in Irish society, may realise the prediction of Pope John Paul II that religious have

> not only a glorious history to remember and to recount but *also a great history still to be accomplished.*[17]

Notes

1. Figures in this paragraph taken from tables compiled by the Council for Research and Development, St. Patrick's College, Maynooth.
2. Corish, P., *The Irish Catholic Experience: A Historical Survey* (Dublin: 1985)
3. Unio Conferentiarum Europae Superiorum Maiorum in which there are 39 Conferences of Religious representing 23 countries. The Secretariat is in Brussels.
4. cf. Corish, *op. cit.*
5. Schneiders, S. 'Congregational Leadership and Spirituality in the Postmodern Era', *Review for Religious* (Jan/Feb 1998), 9.
6. Arbuckle, G., *Strategies for Growth in Religious Life* (New York: 1986), 21.
7. Weafer, J. 'Irish Attitudes towards Religious. A Survey' in *Religious Life Review* Vol. 39 (July/August 2000), 201ff.
8. Kennedy M., reviewing biography of Jean Claude Colin by Donal Kerr in the *Irish Catholic,* March 8 2001.
9. cf. Widdicombe, C. 'Small Communities in Religious Life, Making them Work' (Cambridge: 2001).
10. Pope John Paul II: *Vita Consecrata* 3.
11. *Directory of Retreat Houses and Pastoral Centres in Ireland 2001,* published by the Association of Retreat and Pastoral Centres in Ireland.
12. Pope John Paul II: *Vita Consecrata* 99 (Vatican City, 1996) 180.
13. O'Murchú, D. 'Religious Decline and Revival', *Signum*, 1988, 16:5, 39.
14. Sheldrake, P., 'Raising Historical Perspectives', *The Way*, Supplement 65 (London: 1989), 69.
15. Pope John Paul II: *Vita Consecrata* 3.

16. Fahey, Tony, 'The Catholic Church and Social Policy', *Social Policy in Ireland*, Healy, S. and Reynolds, B., (eds), (Dublin: 1998), p. 248.
17. Pope John Paul II: *Vita Consecrata* 110.

6

Spirituality for Religious in Ireland Today, in the Light of *Vita Consecrata* (1996)

Christopher Dillon OSB

All the usual disclaimers and qualifications need to be made, at the beginning of any study such as this one, because it is inevitably influenced by the presuppositions of a particular spiritual formation. With this in mind, the attempt is being made here, by a monastic author, to limit that bias by taking the post-synodal papal exhortation, *Vita Consecrata* (1996)*, as the yardstick against which to review the statistical analysis of the corpus of religious personnel in Ireland, at the beginning of the third Christian millennium.

Religious personnel in Ireland today have a problem with image. There are all sorts of reasons why that should be so, given the collective sense of responsibility and guilt which has followed the current revelation of scandalous behaviour on the part of some religious, reaching back for many years. Granted

* Bracketed numbers refer to sections of *Vita Consecrata*.

that it is already a problem that image should be in question at all, it is useful to remember that it has been an issue, really, ever since the upheavals of the sixties and the heady days of Vatican II. It is most immediately, if superficially, evident in the elementary matter of religious dress, which was once the unquestioned badge of identity, but also, even if only implicitly, the mark of separation from the rest of men. At the time of writing, it is eschewed by many clergy and religious, on the grounds that it is prejudicially alienating of the public, who associate it with the days of a clerically triumphalist and theocratic society, or that it advertises a negatively conservative view of religious life.

There is no doubt that, in the wake of material advance and social liberalisation since the sixties, there has been a swift and terrible revenge, taken by both the media and the reading public, against the forces in the Church that had effectively controlled the life of ordinary people in Ireland for over a century. The justice or otherwise of the perceptions that have occasioned this reaction, and the absence of historical perspective concerning the interaction of Church and society, are of no consequence at the level of public consciousness. The image has fallen into shape, according to its own logic, and the religious of the land must wear it, like or not, until something happens that changes it. That something will have to be at least as positive and innately attractive in promoting a new appreciation of religious life as recent history has proved to be negative about it. What is at issue is the beauty of God, shown in the life of Christ and visible, today, in the life of his dedicated disciples. That beauty needs no apologia; it needs only to be manifest to be both credible and immediately attractive to the human spirit.

The issue of image has been affected by that of identity, ever since the traditional works of so many charitably oriented orders of women and men were taken over by increasingly socially conscious government programmes. Health and education, which were for so long the prerogative of the well-to-do, have become, in theory at least, the right of every citizen of the European Union, at the expense of the public purse. The once scandalous degradation of the urban poor in Ireland, which made Dublin and Ireland infamous in the Europe of the nineteenth and early twentieth centuries, is now but a subject for sociological history. But, at the time, it moved saintly men and women, such as Ignatius Rice, Mary Aikenhead, Catherine McCauley, Nano Nagle and Theobald Mathew, to works of heroic charity that compare with that of the more widely acknowledged Vincent de Paul, Louise de Marillac and Jane Frances de Chantal in seventeenth century France. What made these Irish initiatives the more remarkable was the speed with which the tiny Catholic bourgeoisie, only recently enjoying religious freedom, should have been able to galvanise its energies in favour of elementary social justice. It was as though a gushing spring had been released in the Irish religious psyche, which was energised to transform Irish society from its state of poverty and degradation to being an increasingly self-confident democracy in the community of nations.

But there was more. No sooner had these religiously inspired orders of teachers and nurses identified their quarry at home, and carved out their territory, so to speak, than the urge to bring the same benefits to the colonies of the British Empire evoked the long dormant energy of the missionary spirit. The Maynooth Mission to China, the Sisters of Our Lady of Apostles and Mary Martin's Medical Missionaries of Mary, in the early years of the last century, made a distinctive addition to the existing cohorts heading for the mission territories. It is not so long since one could jest, with some pride, that the largest Irish exports were Guinness's stout and Catholic missionaries.

It is no secret that the convent or monastery once opened the door to further education and a social security for some who might not otherwise have had the opportunity to achieve them. But the opening up of Irish society and the opportunities that have been ushered in by prosperity have changed all that. Not only are there now a variety of very attractive options available to our relatively well educated younger generations, but there no longer exists the kind of socio-religious context of support that once prompted so many to 'take up the cross', in the service of the institutional Church. There is a sense in which the option for religious life is absolutely counter-cultural, today, where it would have met with approval and admiration half a century ago. In this much changed society, the problems of identity and image of the religious man or woman have merged to become a crisis of *raison d'être*. But this is true only insofar as the *raison d'être* of these so-called apostolic religious is to be defined in terms of their traditional apostolate, whether that be in healthcare or in the education of the underprivileged, for example.

The very material transformation of contemporary Irish society has had its peculiar effects on the components of that same religious psyche. On the one hand, the crying social needs of earlier years, on the home front at least, are now not at all so urgent. Indeed, there is a sense in which the involvement of religious in what used to be their *raison d'être* is sometimes represented as taking jobs out of the hands of lay-people who are trying to earn enough to raise their families. Even the efforts in the missionary field have met with the criticism that the post-colonial indigènes are better left undisturbed by the questionable benefits of western culture and unencumbered by the complications of a Christian conscience. On the other hand, it is also true that the cohorts of young men and women, who once swelled the ranks of the religious, are no longer queuing up to make that sort of choice for their lives.

If there is any truth in this analysis, it is significant only to the degree that the motivation for making a religious commitment in that context may have been mixed with opportunism. But it reflects, as well, a certain social complacency, which tolerated vocational mediocrity and a degree of religious formalism. The astringent character of contemporary Irish culture guarantees that no such opportunism or formalism is likely to be operative today. Instead there is likely to be a bracing challenge to anything like religious commitment, which will certainly serve to purify its motivation.

This is where *Vita Consecrata* has so much to offer, in terms of its analysis of religious life in the overall mission of the Church and of its canonisation of the unqualified Christian vocation to follow Christ, according to the evangelical counsels that characterised his earthly life. Its basic insight is to remind all religious men and women, of whatever inspiration, that their primary reason for being is precisely the 'prolongation of the humanity of Christ' in the world (76). They have accepted 'the mystery of Christ, lived within the Church' as being definitive of their own particular relationship with Him, characterised by the practice of the evangelical counsels (16). It is a basic tenet of this document that the various charisms that have inspired this specificity of Christian commitment 'have helped to make the mission and mystery of the Church shine forth and, in doing so, have contributed to the renewal of society' (1).

In the spirit of the return to the sources, which characterised so much of the renewal of the 1960s, 'faithfulness to the charism of the founder or foundress' (36/37) is cited as the surest way to keep in touch with tradition and the spirit of the Church. But, if the situation of need that inspired the foundation of a particular congregation has changed, it is not always easy to see how this 'faithfulness' is to be fruitfully maintained. At the same time, it is undeniable that Jesus' dictum, 'The poor you will always have with you', remains as valid today, as it was when he first uttered it. The margins of our society are as wide and as populous as ever they were, despite our membership of the group of desirable destinations for the refugees of the world. At the same time, the 'preferential option for the poor' is now generally accepted as an essential feature of any genuinely apostolic religious life (82).

There is a repeated and slightly troubling reference, in *Vita Consecrata*, to the 'objective superiority' of religious life, precisely because of its process and goal of configuration to Christ (18;32). Contemporary religious tend to shun any such value-judgement, because it seems both to re-introduce the pedestal on which religious have been perched and to ignore the universal application of the 'call to holiness', which is a pearl of the thinking of *Lumen Gentium* and Vatican II. But it is uncomfortably true that this mention of superiority poses a challenge to religious to appreciate and acknowledge the demands of the commitment to Christ that they once made, 'in the first fervour of their conversion' (Rule of Benedict). The quality of the life of the typical religious should be such as to shine out, like a lamp on a pedestal, to occasion not admiration of the individual but reverence for the God who has inspired it. The contrary tendency of melting into the crowd, which is actually a characteristic of some congregational charisms, may include for others a not entirely praiseworthy desire for the freedom of anonymity. We have all experienced the inconvenience of being marked out and of being wearied by unwanted attention. Maybe, we need to be willing to be more visible, more identifiable, for Him whose servants we are. How else is the world to be brought to believe (Jn 17:21; 1 Jn 5:4)?

The specificity of religious life is to be identified in the special relationship that Jesus established with some of his disciples, in the call to follow him (14). While it is clear that this call applies to all Christians, the person consecrated to living by the evangelical counsels makes 'a specific acceptance of the mystery of Christ, lived within the Church', in terms that should demonstrate that the incarnate Son of God is the infinite beauty, which alone can satisfy the human heart (16). This, then, becomes the basis of the radical dedication of the self to the Father, after the manner of the Son, who came not to do his own will but the will of the Father. The task, thereafter, is one of witness to Gospel values, for the benefit of the baptised, who must be constantly reminded that the world cannot be transfigured other than by the spirit of the Beatitudes (33). The fruit of this work, with its renewed commitment to holiness of life, is nothing less than transfiguration or, better, a configuration to Christ, by means of a continual experience of conversion.

The centre-piece of *Vita Consecrata* is significantly entitled, *Signum Fraternitatis*. This builds on the phenomenon of community life as a 'God-enlightened space' (42), which can transform human relationships to a new kind of solidarity. A collaborative vision of the Church is proposed, here, in a manner that seeks to transcend distinctions of the diocesan, regular and lay vocation to holiness, in the service of the Kingdom of God. There is particular emphasis on the connection between religious and the diocesan Church, so that the holiness of life, which is the business of religious, may be seen to be a leaven in the Church as well as in society at large. In a call to 'feel with the Church', *sentire cum Ecclesia* (46), there is an appeal for a generous appreciation of the variety of needs and vocational roles within the Church, in a manner that seeks to draw together and re-group its combined resources. The candid acknowledgement of the qualities that are peculiar to other vocations enables each to rejoice in the gift of the other to the whole Church. If these are to be sources of mutual enrichment, and they should be, it is essential that each different charism be faithfully nurtured and maintained within its own tradition. There seems to be a providential thrust from the laity, in this direction, with the numbers of lay associates who are ready to devote themselves to the work and welfare of individual communities. Sometimes, these lay associates reflect the spirit of the original charism more obviously than their consecrated fellows!

While this welcome development may appear to compensate for a general decline in numbers of consecrated religious, it should not be taken as the necessary way of the future, to the prejudice of discipline and specific formation, particularly on-going formation of individuals and communities. One reason for this, quite apart from the good of individual communities, is the obligation to keep aglow and visible the individual aspects of the beauty of Christ in each charism, which may attract those who are searching for them. Unlikely though it may seem, in these times of difficulty, there are men and women, young and not so young, who are waiting to hear the invitation, 'Come and see' (Jn.1:39), and that with a view to something closer than mere association with the congregation.

The final section of *Vita Consecrata* focuses on the work of loving service, which is the manifestation of God's love at work in the world. The essentially missionary character of the Church is evoked to make the point that the primary task of the religious is to make Christ present to the world (72). Something of that New Testament evangelism that had the disciples braving the wrath of the authorities, by preaching 'all about this new life' in the Temple (Acts, 5:17-21), is needed to achieve that prophetic joy that speaks to the world of the new life in Christ. The innate value of this life needs to be proclaimed, not so much by speaking about it as by allowing its holiness to shine through the lived example of communities and individuals; but by communities, rather than by individuals. These Christians need to be recognised as such by the practical love they have for one another. Indeed, the process of being conformed to Christ parallels the growth in awareness of that mission. The explicit identification, here, of dialogue, as 'the new name of charity' in the Church (74), presents a new and interesting challenge to this missionary task. If we are to engage with others constructively, at any level, we must be both well-informed and credible messengers, sensitive to the challenges of contemporary society and as willing to listen as we are ready to speak. An essential ingredient of this engagement is a loving familiarity with the Word of God, in the regular practice of *lectio divina,* which is a genuine source of supernatural intuition. We must be not only able to communicate the word of God's love, but our manner of life should be such as to exude it as 'a prolongation of the humanity of Christ' (ibid.).

Intrinsic to this love, lived in Christ, is the preferential option for the poor, the disadvantaged and the marginalised. The refugees, the aged and the victims of new infectious diseases seem to fill these categories, today; and their number is growing. While the Welfare State has moved into so much of the territory that has been the traditional bailiwick of religious congregations, the poor are always with us, beyond the reach of the most diligent offices of the State. Health and education are provided, up to a point, but society is rapidly coming to appreciate that that point is soon reached when the public purse finds it is inadequate to the needs of a service that has been supplied by Christian dedication. There is a constant need for religious who are dedicated to the care of the sick. There is just as much need for the presence of religious in the world of education, at every level. In our rapidly secularised society, there is the newly identified need of the evangelisation of culture, which demands sophisticated and specialised training, if an effective dialogue with the world is to be maintained. There is an obvious and pressing application of this principle in the ecumenical field, in this country.

There is a focus, here, on community life that is significant, given that so many congregations have experienced difficulty with, and have consequently jettisoned, a style of community life that was suitable to monks and nuns, rather than to apostolic religious. This inheritance reflected an attitude to authority and obedience, which took small account of the social revolutions of the twentieth century, in the western world, while it tended to canonise the practical customs of an earlier age as though they were of scriptural significance. The recommendation, then, to look again at the value of the collective witness of the common life poses a particular challenge to the many religious, who have adopted a looser structure of life. The ideals of the Acts of the Apostles and the early Christian community are proposed to us, again, in the familiar terms of the evangelical counsels, with a view to recovering that prophetic stance, in society, which speaks of the primacy of the love of Christ in the Christian life (84). They pose a suitable challenge to the idolatry of sexuality, materialism and individualism, in our western culture, and their abuse of personal freedom. This last is particularly true of obedience in community, which is so much at variance with the Zeitgeist. But it must be said that this very visible commitment to the spiritual life is its own attractive advertisement to the many who are in search of absolute values.

The task for religious, today, remains what it has always been, namely, the celebration and the demonstration of God's love in his world. Religious men and women should be that leaven in society that attracts people in general to the things of God. As in the days of early Rome, when the followers of Christ were identified for the love they showed, so must it be again in our day. The credibility of religious life, the credibility of the Church, itself, is at stake. The sense of unease in this regard, which is abroad at the moment, is a measure of the extent to which personal conversion and collective witness is so vital. The task is an individual one, which will bear its best fruit in the quality of community life, as reservoirs of holiness. After that, it remains for the beauty of God's love to work its own magic in the world. The only possible obstacle to this is the lack of confidence on the part of consecrated men and women in their ability, under God, to make a difference in the world.

7

Setting the Changes in Historical Context

Dermot Keogh

Nostalgia is a poor guide to an understanding of the past. But the 'facts' produced by a survey, unless read carefully, may prove to be an equally unreliable guide to future trends. What, in the history and present reality of religious life and religious traditions in Ireland, does not easily lend itself to quantitative evaluation? That, at the very outset, needs to be stated with emphasis.

It is relatively easy to quantify the number of Irish religious working at home and abroad. It is particularly difficult to *measure* aspects of the contemporary history of religion and of religious in society. How is it possible to capture the extent to which the ideas and the spirituality of the major founders of the different religious orders, mediated through the work of generations of religious, has and continues to influence the value systems of many individuals working in those societies? That may not be at issue in this particular survey. But it should be a major consideration in attempting to evaluate the *strength* of religious life in Ireland today.

What any historian interpreting a survey must first establish is the frame of reference on which the report is based. What were the questions that were not asked? What was not tested by the survey?

Unfortunately the study has no comparative international dimension. This may not have been part of the original commissioning brief. But the absence of a comparative context, even in the footnotes, in my view weakens the work. Ironically many of the orders included in the survey are transnational in structure and lend themselves quite easily to regional/national comparison.

It might have been useful for the survey to have also provided a breakdown between Irish foundations, European continental foundations and US and Third World foundations working on this island.

It is a source of disappointment that the survey has been reduced in scope and, unlike the 1989 research, does not include data on 23 non-conference members many of which have large memberships, viz. Society of African Missions, Missionaries for Africa, Columban Fathers, Mill Hill Fathers, St Patrick's Missionary Society, etc.

It would have been most useful, too, to have had included in the survey a statistical overview of the number of religious in the country since the foundation of the Irish Free State and Northern Ireland.

I also found missing from the study a breakdown of figures between different categories of religious orders, for example, pastoral or contemplative.

None of these comments are meant to question the professionalism or detract from the importance of the commissioned survey. It provides a very valuable snapshot of the numerical strength of religious life in Ireland in 1999. The conclusions that must be drawn ought to have a sobering effect on both members of religious orders and lay Catholics alike.

Some 77 percent of religious in Ireland are sisters. Clerical religious are 16 percent and brothers make up seven percent of the total. There are 10,975 religious working and/or living in Ireland compared with 17,373 in 1981 and 15,634 in 1989. The survey also computes the number of Irish religious working abroad. This brings the figures up to 13,393 compared with 23,308 in 1981.

The rate of decline, reported by the survey, is striking; there has been a 29 percent decline of religious (4,659) since 1989 and the rate of decline since 1981 has been 37 per cent (6,398). The survey finds, however, that the total decrease may be nearer to 3,000 when the number of deaths, departures and entrants are counted. The numbers of entrants and departures more or less balanced each other out. Entrants to Irish orders are very often recruited abroad and, should they remain, are unlikely to minister in Ireland.

Two interrelated factors give further cause for concern – the relative lack of recruits to orders and the age profile of Irish religious. The survey finds that just over two thirds of Irish religious are aged 60 years of age or over. Only eleven per cent are less than 50 years of age. This trend is most pronounced in sisters' congregations where seven in ten sisters are sixty years or over. Only seven per cent are less than 50 years of age. When these figures are broken down, a mere two per cent of all three categories of religious are under twenty nine years of age and 3.2 percent between thirty and thirty nine years of age. Clerical religious congregations, unlike orders of sisters and brothers, have twenty-eight per cent under the age of fifty.

However, it ought not to be concluded that the younger religious are working in Ireland. The survey shows that seventy-eight per cent of those under the age of twenty-nine are posted outside of the country. There are 920 members of Irish religious orders working in Africa; 713 in Britain and that excludes Northern Ireland; 178 in the rest of Europe; 209 in the USA and Canada and 398 listed as 'other'. This latter category includes Central and South America.

The survey demonstrates an apparent asymmetry in the distribution of religious in Ireland, with 52 per cent stationed in Leinster, 26 per cent in Munster, ten per cent in Connacht and 11 per cent in Ulster. When this is broken down further, it is revealed that just over half of religious working in Ireland are located in four counties: Dublin, Cork, Galway and Limerick. This deployment reflects the historical commitments of those religious orders and this now calls for major re-evaluation.

But, amid the gloomy atmosphere of declining vocations and aging communities, it is well to single out the response of congregation leaders to the question 'Do you believe religious life has a future in Ireland? Two percent replied 'no'; six percent responded 'don't know' and 92 per cent said 'yes'. I am assuming that that reply was emphatic rather than haltering and tentative. I also assume that that reply was a response based on the deeply held conviction that the religious life as it has survived since the Middle Ages is undergoing radical change and that it will emerge mostly in a new form, or take many new forms, in the twenty-first century. The survey finds that a majority of 74 per cent of congregation leaders 'are either enthusiastic or hopeful' towards the future of religious life. Of the remaining 26 per cent opinions among congregation leaders range from 'somewhat hopeful' to 'not hopeful' about religious life. The survey further concludes:

> More than nine in ten leaders believe religious life has a future in Ireland, even if for many of them, the future is different from its present form. Many leaders feel that religious life will survive in smaller groups that are immersed in local communities with a simpler and less institutionalised lifestyle.

I read the above as a prediction rooted in hope rather than a mere aspiration. The survey has been constructed to provide a response that yields the genuine feelings and outlook of many congregation leaders. Otherwise, this section of the report might be compared to the forlorn exhortations a football manager whose team is trailing ten-nil at half time.

But the responses do not betray any sense of hopelessness. Congregation leaders mentioned 'continuity of mission' frequently in the survey. They believe that the journey of their respective congregations is not yet finished. Historically, religious life was cyclical but indestructible. New life is emerging. This appears to be a view widely enough shared to be mentioned 25 times by congregation leaders.

The lack of vocations and the high percentage of male and female religious over sixty must be balanced against that strong spirit of innovation. There are those who appear lost and confused in a crisis where no end is in sight. It is quite surprising that so few in the survey have laid emphasis on an unwillingness to take risks as contributing to the current state of affairs – a reticence about launching out into the deep. That point will be returned to later in this short essay.

Professional historical analysis, unlike nostalgic reflections about 'the way things were', may not yield comforting and soothing results for religious orders in Ireland now in a phase of apparent decline. It might be helpful to frame the options facing the future of those in religious congregations in Ireland in an historical context. Why and how do religious congregations find themselves facing the contemporary challenges quantified in the survey?

Is there a specificity unique to the Irish situation or is it merely a question of Irish religious having to face the same situation as many of the same orders confronted a few decades earlier in Britain, the Commonwealth, Canada, the United States and in continental Europe? Is Ireland merely a few decades behind other countries in the process referred to as Western modernisation? Answers to those questions will not be found in a survey. But it is possible to make the mistake of having the deterministic secularising model of modernisation in mind when reading this report. I would like to postulate other possible outcomes. Here it is necessary to make a number of historical observations.

Since the foundation of the Irish Free State and Northern Ireland, male and female religious have played a prominent role in the development of the educational and social infrastructure. Born out of civil war, the resources at the disposal of the government of William T. Cosgrave in the 1920s proved to be very limited. The more grandiose schemes and vision of the revolutionary period between 1916 and 1921 were set aside as the Irish government set about securing the survival of the state. It faced the struggle to provide popular legitimacy for the new government throughout the 1920s against a sustained opposition – political and subversive – from those who opposed the Treaty.

The Catholic Church played a leading role in helping the new political leaders, William T. Cosgrave (1922-32) and Eamon de Valera (1932-48); ensure the legitimisation of that state. The hierarchy was vociferous in its support of the Treaty and of the government during the civil war between 1922 and 1923. Confronted by the poverty of the 1920s and 1930s, the Catholic Church lent its unstinting support to the building of the state. Religious orders played a prominent role in the pastoral life of the church. But nuns, priests and brothers were already heavily committed to the running of schools and hospitals. They were also responsible for the running of orphanages, and industrial schools which looked after over 6,000 children per annum.

In many cases, the religious simply continued their commitment to the running of hospitals, schools and other institutions. This commitment dated back in many cases to the nineteenth century. The new Irish state was as anxious as the British state had once been to ensure that the religious orders continue their commitment to the running of schools and hospitals. Irish nationalism reinforced a philosophy of pastoral concern.

Neither the government of William T. Cosgrave nor that of Eamon de Valera sought, in the case of industrial schools and orphanages, to request religious to stand back from the commitments entered into under the British to run those institutions. The orders were given wide powers to carry out their custodial roles in industrial schools and orphanages.

Vocations in the 1920s and 1930s to religious orders were plentiful and there was no shortage of work for those religious who ministered in Ireland. Members of the hierarchy were anxious for religious to take on new assignments. Orders, with a strong flow of vocations, were in a position to respond with generosity. This was particularly the case in the areas of health care and education.

John Charles McQuaid, Archbishop of Dublin from 1940 until 1972, was not alone on the bench of bishops in his desire to encourage religious to deploy their resources in the running of institutions. This was partially motivated by a strong fear of the power of the state. He did not mistrust leaders like William T. Cosgrave and Eamon de Valera. But he did fear what might happen in the distant future in the event of a secular, anti-clerical government coming to power in Ireland were the state to become too strong.

In a climate of Catholic institutional expansionism, a phase which lasted into the 1960s, the question must be posed about the extent to which religious orders were planning for the future or were merely responding to the frequent requests from members of the hierarchy to meet certain diocesan needs. Here I am speculating. But it must have been difficult for a congregation leader to plan for the long term when so many demands were being made to answer the needs of dioceses in Ireland and abroad.

There is also another consideration. Congregation leaders were confronted with the challenge of having to train and provide personnel for the running of a multiplicity of institutions. Indeed, religious orders may often have found themselves engaged in work for which they were neither trained nor suited. Here I am thinking particularly about primary or secondary teachers being put into the area of running an orphanage or an industrial school.

The McQuaid model of Church was contingent upon the continued and plentiful supply of religious to provide the necessary support for the running of a range of institutions – the buildings themselves giving a distinctive character to the majority of Irish towns. There was a convent school on one side of the town and a Christian Brothers school on the other. In some cases, in the big cities in particular, there would be a number of religious-run hospitals. There were specialist educational institutions for those suffering from disabilities, homes for unmarried mothers, orphanages and industrial schools.

How many leaders of religious congregations viewed the range of their respective order's institutional commitments in the 1960s and wondered how much longer it would be possible to sustain pastoral engagement at such a high level?

Will the archives of the orders reveal a record of concern about the relevance of certain commitments and about the ability of the order to live up to the demands of Church and State?

At another level, will documents in religious archives reflect an anxiety about the extent to which orders found themselves trapped into sustaining historical commitments even when such commitments were not in accord with the mission propounded by the founder?

Perhaps it was a belief in Irish Catholic particularism that sustained religious leaders in the mistaken belief that Ireland would be different from the rest of Western Europe? This is not to concede an acceptance of a deterministic view of modernisation – economic prosperity to be followed automatically by a decline of religion.

But that sense of Irish particularism may have lulled religious leaders into a sense of false security; the mission of religious orders would continue determined by the needs of society, the state and the hierarchy. Ireland was different. The Irish church did not need to change. After all, this was Ireland. Many religious orders built in the 1960s for expansion working on the assumption that high vocation rates of the early 1960s would be sustained through the following decades. Yet, by the 1980s and 1990s, change had occurred. The Church from the 1920s had been like a river in spate. It flowed into every corner and cranny. Religious were overextended in their commitments by the 1970s.

Reviewing the commitment of the Irish Church in the 1960s to the running of a national educational and medical infrastructure, there may have been congregation leaders who anticipated that a rapid change in the fortunes of Catholicism would leave orders in a vulnerable position. Like an advancing army spread out over a vast distance, any sudden change in fortune meant that decisions would have to be made about what to hold and what to abandon. The Catholic Church suffered such a sudden reverse in the 1980s. The Archbishop McQuaid era was over.

Many orders have been attempting to evaluate long-term pastoral commitment in the light of falling vocations and in the certain knowledge that there is no new generation coming behind to take over from the religious just over two thirds of whom are over sixty. Is this a crisis for religious? It may be seen as such if the role of the orders is viewed in a static way. But it must be asked whether religious orders were too slow to change the nature of their pastoral and professional commitments in the second half of the twentieth century? Were they too comfortable in their respective historical roles to the detriment of being able to evaluate and plan for new pastoral challenges in the latter part of the twentieth century? Why was there a reluctance to hand over schools and hospitals over to lay management? Why did orders not hand over to the state the running of industrial schools, orphanages and other institutions? Such an option was not possible given the resources at the disposal of the state at the time may be a perfectly adequate and accurate reply. But it does not fully explain the reticence to review pastoral missions and plan for the future.

In the first decade of the twenty-first century, the hard decisions may no longer be put on the long finger. Religious orders are now obliged to confront the possibility that some may not survive the coming twenty or thirty years. If it is accepted that the institutional phase of religious life in Ireland is now going to continue to exist on a much smaller scale, then new possibilities are opened up. Doomsday need not necessarily be nigh.

This may be the period to rediscover the founding mission of an order in a new historical context. Creative responses will ensure that the intellectual and spiritual traditions of an order is carried on in new forms.

The challenge for many orders is to focus on the need to put in place structures to ensure the continuity of the spirit of Ignatius, Dominic, Benedict, Bonaventure, Francis, Vincent, Edmund Ignatius Rice, Clare, Ursula, Teresa, Mary Martin, Nano Nagle, Catherine McAuley, Mary Aikenhead, etc. That will almost certainly mean having to entrust the continuation of those theological and spiritual traditions mainly to laymen and women.

While the modalities of discovering new religious forms is not a subject for this short essay, the embedding of the diverse religious traditions in Irish society will *not* be achieved by the founding of secretive, closed lay groups who form a new elite or elect. One of the most significant dangers facing Irish Catholicism today is the temptation for those in authority to look to 'loyalists' who feel most comfortable working under a cloak of secrecy in order to preserve the future of the Catholic Church.

In a pluralist, multi-cultural and multi-ethnic society that is Ireland today, the onus on religious is to deepen their skills for dialogue and discussions with people of different faiths and none. There is also a need to develop new structures for the transmission of the gospel message. The succession of tribunals dealing with the meat industry, planning and development, etc., gives pause to any one in Ireland wishing to speak nostalgically about the perfection of a past that is no more.

What I wish to argue here is that the diminution in the size of religious communities in Ireland is not necessarily the prelude to extinction. It simply provides the context in which a long-overdue evaluation of the role of religious in Irish society should take place. The continued witness of Irish religious, projecting another thirty years ahead, will not depend upon the extent to which orders continue to keep schools, hospitals and other institutions under their control. It is much more important to ensure that such institutions continue to operate according to gospel values in tandem with the spirit of the founders interpreted in the light of a radically changed, and changing, historical context.

8

Money, Spirituality and the Religious Congregations

Tony Fahey

Coming up to Confirmation time in Tullamore in 1841, Mother M. Anne, the reverend mother of St Joseph's Mercy Convent, invited Rev. Theobald Mathew to preach on the theme of temperence at the Confirmation ceremony for her pupils.* The convent had been founded five years earlier and in 1841 the convent school was bringing its first group of pupils to Confirmation. However, when the diocesan bishop, Dr John Cantwell, heard of the invitation, he instructed Mother M. Anne to withdraw it, which she was obliged to do. Dr Cantwell's reasoning was that the main local benefactor to the convent was a distiller, as were some other prominent Catholics in the King's County, and he felt that 'it would be injudicious to excite them'. When Mother M. Anne communicated her disappointment at this turn of events to Catherine McAuley,

*This and the following paragraphs refer to extracts from the annals of St Joseph's Convent as reprinted in pp. 65-76 of Mary C. Sullivan (1997), *Catherine McAuley and the Tradition of Mercy*, Notre Dame, Indiana: University of Notre Dame Press and Dublin: Four Courts Press.

the head of the Mercy Congregation (who was to die later in the same year), she got some sympathy but little of the expression of irritation at the bishop she might have expected. The tone of Catherine's comments, as recorded in the convent annals, suggests that she regarded the bishop's instruction as a useful lesson in humility and obedience, and otherwise 'supposed that the bishop hoped the cause of temperance would go ahead quietly'.

A year earlier, a critical decision had been taken in the same convent that was to have far reaching consequences for the role of the Sisters of Mercy in Ireland, as well as for the evolution of the Irish education system. Catherine McAuley was on one of her periodic visits from Dublin to the convent. During her stay, she received a petition from some Catholic families in Tullamore that the convent open a 'pension school' for girls from respectable families. Catherine's initial reaction was to say no. The constitution of her congregation, the ink of which was hardly dry on the page, had laid down that its principal social objectives were the instruction of poor girls, the visitation of the sick and the 'protection of distressed women of good character' (that is, the provision of accommodation for unmarried mothers). These objectives did not extend to the education of middle-class girls, and in any event Catherine McAuley pointed out that congregations such as the Loreto and Ursuline sisters already provided such a service. However, the petitioners persisted, saying that the Loreto and Ursuline schools were too far away and beyond their means, and they needed a local service. In response, and apparently without much further thought, Catherine changed her mind and 'at once acquiesced and sanctioned' the setting up of a pension school.

This decision, so lightly taken, proved to be momentous for the Sisters of Mercy. It opened the way for the congregation to enter the field of fee-paying secondary education in Ireland. (The founding of the National Education system in 1831, which was designed to provide state-funded universal primary education, meant that the distinction between 'poor schools' and pension schools at primary level had already begun to lose its former significance by 1841.) The entry into secondary education in turn eventually placed them at the centre of an important aspect of middle-class and lower middle-class life in Ireland. When added to their rapidly growing role in primary education, it made them a major force in the Irish education system. However, it also departed from the spirit of the congregation's own constitution, since it extended the sisters' educational efforts to the mainstream population as well as the poor – to the extent, perhaps, that the former soon dislodged the latter at the centre of the congregation's attentions. Furthermore, this departure was sanctioned by Catherine McAuley, who had hitherto placed so much emphasis on the primacy of the poor in the congregation's social activities.

When these two episodes occurred, religious congregations had not yet assumed the importance in the pastoral and social service work of the Church that they were later to achieve. There were then about 1,500 female religious in Ireland (as recorded in the 1851 census of population). This was a big increase from the count of 200 nuns in the country that the *Catholic Directory* had provided in 1800, but it was only the beginning of a remarkable longterm growth. That growth continued until the late 1960s, by which time there was close to 18,000 religious sisters in Ireland, the majority of whom were engaged in the provision of high quality services in education, health and social care. Because the congregations subsidised these services out of their own resources (which they were able to do on account of the spartan lifestyle of the sisters) they were provided at a cost to the consumer and tax-payer that was well below their real value.

Since the late 1960s, as the figures compiled by John Weafer elsewhere in this volume confirm, decline in numbers has been as rapid as was the growth in the nineteenth and early twentieth centuries. Looking at the age distribution of nuns today, it is likely that by the middle of the twenty-first century, many of the smaller congregations will have disappeared and total numbers among those remaining will have fallen back below the level of 1,500 attained in the middle of the nineteenth. Among the male religious orders and congregations, the picture is similar though on a smaller scale, as their numbers at their peak were only a fraction (in the region of a quarter or so) of those of the female congregations.

With the cycle in its present downward phase, many congregations are looking back to their beginnings in the search for pointers to the role they should now adopt. They have had much discussion about their roots and the spirit of their founders and much reflection on how those might be rediscovered and adapted for the world today. In some instances, this has given rise to a shift to the left on social issues, inspired by the concern for the poor expressed by founders, as re-interpreted within the framework of post-1960s liberation theology and its call to the faithful to make an 'option for the poor'.

It is in this context that the episodes in St Joseph's Mercy convent in Tullamore in 1841 become relevant. Their significance goes beyond Catherine McAuley and the Sisters of Mercy, as they reflect realities that shaped the social role and religious character of Catholic congregations generally since the early nineteenth century. In one sense, it is unfair to highlight these two events as they present the religious and the wider Church in an unflattering light. They hint at moral weakness and uncertainty of purpose. They conflict with the traditional – and much justified – reputation for drive and single-minded devotion to the faith which is usually associated with the religious founders. They say nothing of the energy, dedication and quiet heroism that so often characterised the work of thousands religious in Ireland down through the decades, nor of the genuine inspiration which Catherine McAuley and other pioneers like her offered her followers.

On the other hand, if the religious today are looking back to the early years of their congregations in the search for guides to the future, it is as well that they see those early years from more than one angle. Figures such as Catherine McAuley, Nano Nagle and Edmund Rice pioneered a new, successful and impressive mode of religious action in the early nineteenth century, but they did so in the context of their times. It is important to appreciate what that entailed, since there may be limits to the degree to which the founders can be lifted out of their context and looked to as a source of fresh impetus for the religious life today.

What, then, were the realities that the incidents in Tullamore in 1841 point to?

The distiller episode reminds us first of all that money talks – and even saintly reverend mothers must listen to what it says. Congregations had to have a financial basis for their mission, and religious founders such as Catherine McAuley were pragmatic enough to recognise that that imperative imposed limits on what they could do and say. In the Tullamore instance, it was the bishop of the diocese who reminded the sisters in St Joseph's convent that one of the hands that fed them was a distiller's, and that it would be therefore injudicious to provide a platform to a passionate temperance preacher on their first major ceremonial occasion. However, while the reverend mother in St Joseph's was slow to absorb that fact, Catherine McAuley was not – and had her disposition been otherwise it is unlikely that the congregation she founded and stamped with her character would have grown, as it eventually did, into one of the largest in the Catholic world. In her defence, and in Dr Cantwell's, it might be said that had St Joseph's convent bitten the distiller's hand on that occasion, it might subsequently have foundered for the want of financial support. However immediately satisfying its moral stance might have been, the congregation's potential for serving the Church or helping the poor would therefore have been lost for good. The incident indicates, therefore, that dilemmas such as these confronted Catherine McAuley just as much as any of her successors. Saintliness of character on its own was not enough to transcend the need for compromise which those dilemmas demanded, so that much accommodation with an unjust world inevitably resulted.

In time, many religious congregations in Ireland gained a considerable degree of independence from benevolent donations and popular subscription as sources of income, since many of their members became in effect state-salaried teachers, nurses and care-workers in what continued to be religious owned and run schools, hospitals and other social services. This gave them a degree of economic security and of economic independence from the rest of the Catholic Church that was not enjoyed by their counterparts in many other countries. Even then, however, they had to remain acceptable to a broad public in order to retain the large clientele for their social services, which was the ultimate source of their finance viability. That in turn drew them towards a centrist position in social affairs and limited their ability to act as critics and forces for social reform in the world they lived in.

This points to a further reality hinted at by the episodes in Tullamore, namely that neither Catherine McAuley nor any of the other successful religious founders of the nineteenth century in Ireland were social radicals, nor even social thinkers of any depth. It may be satisfying today to represent them as social activists who happened to be in the religious life but the reality was that they were religious ascetics who pursued the path of spiritual perfection through pastoral and social service work for the Church. Philanthropy did figure in their outlook, they had strong humanitarian impulses, and followed through on those impulses with remarkable energy. But philanthropy was a means to the ends of personal spiritual perfection and the winning of souls for the faith, not a primary goal in its own right.

As manifestations of the long tradition of organised, active asceticism within the Church, the religious congregations can hardly be criticised for ordering their priorities in this way. However, these priorities did have implications for their social mission. They had the consequence, for example, that the congregations' social engagement, impressive in scale though it was, was, in a sense, an afterthought: it did not involve anything by way of systematic reflection on the social issues of the day and in consequence was characterised by a lack of intellectually-grounded social awareness. Religious congregations in the Catholic Church generally (with the partial exception of the more intellectually oriented male orders such as the Jesuits) made little contribution to intellectual debates on questions of poverty and social justice in nineteenth-century Europe and gave little indication of interest in or understanding of those debates. In Ireland, the silence of the religious in systematic social commentary was all the more notable because of their prominence in so many fields of social service. This helps explain why Catherine McAuley could so easily acquiesce in her congregation's move into pension schools. The congregation's orientation to the poor, which that move did much to dilute, was not grounded in a consciously worked out commitment to social justice nor in any reflection on what social justice might entail. Rather, it was simply one form of service to the faith among a wide range of possibilities. Other selections from that range – such as, in this instance, the education of middle-class girls – could be added when local conditions in the Church required it. From an ecclesiastical point of view, such an addition to their remit was wholly justified, since in the nineteenth century, as in every other era of the Church's history, the faith could survive and expand only if it percolated into the middle and upper reaches of society as well as among the poor.

The Mercy congregation's underlying priorities in this area were reflected in the balance between social and spiritual concerns in the core articulation of its nature and mission found in its constitution. Social objectives are dealt with in a few short, bald paragraphs in that document, presented without any contextual reference to a broader social analysis. The bulk of the document consists of an extensive treatment of various aspects of spiritual practice and congregational life and draws on the rich traditions of the Church in those areas. In the case of the Sisters of Mercy, as of all the congregations founded in this period, it is clear from the balance between social and spiritual analysis in all their central documents where the focus of their reflective energies were directed.

The work of the Catholic religious congregations undoubtedly raised the standard of social service provision in Ireland in the nineteenth century and brought enormous benefit to wide sections of the population. But it did so in a way that reflected and even reinforced existing social hierarchies. The religious congregations provided elite schools as well as poor schools and exclusive services for the wealthy as well as broadly provided services for the less well off. Their purpose was to strengthen the Catholic ethos and religious commitment of all levels of Catholic society, not to transform relationships between the rich and the poor. As social provision by the state expanded in the twentieth century, the religious congregations were more often opposed to rather than in favour of reforms that would distribute educational and health services more equitably. Those congregations most oriented to populist provision, such as the Sisters of Mercy and Irish Christian Brothers, eventually found themselves more identified with the lower middle classes than those at the very bottom of the social scale and even in their founders' lifetimes had already begun to acquire the disciplinary, containment role that subsequently characterised their relationship to the marginalised who came into their care.

From the perspective of today, there is no doubt that the early years of the congregations in the nineteenth century still carry some inspiriational clout. The founders and their early followers created so much out of so little that it would be hard not to be impressed. However, in many respects, a gulf has opened up between their world and that faced by religious today. That gulf is so wide that it may be more difficult to reach across than religious today generally sometimes seem to believe.

One things that is different now is the utterly changed economic and financial circumstances facing the congregations today. Paradoxically, as the religious decline in numbers they can shed many of the worries about money that so preoccupied and constrained their founders. The property assets of the congregations and the combined pension entitlements of their members amount to a significant body of wealth and will be enough to see them adequately through the coming decades. Since their numbers are dwindling, they have no obligation to invest in their own future, either by providing for the training of large numbers of new members or by building up further facilities. In fact, they are now widely off-loading property they no longer need nor can cope with, so that they are now as likely to be faced with an excess rather than a shortage of cash flows.

This circumstance on its own transforms the relationship between the congregations and the world around them: the hand that feeds them is their own and they no longer need to defer to external sensitivites in order to guarantee their financial viability. That freedom from financial constraint provides an economic underpinning for the social radicalism they now increasingly espouse. However, while Catherine McAuley might have had some sympathy for the new social conscience of the congregations, she would not necessarily have looked benignly on the retreat from service to the better off which it entails. Nor might she be impressed by the view sometimes expressed today that religious are no longer needed in, say, mainstream primary or secondary schooling because the State now makes adequate provision in these areas. She might feel, rather, that the religious are needed in the schools more than ever as the education system sheds its spiritual ethos and threatens a reign of godlessness that she would be horrified to contemplate.

Aside from a difference of emphasis between social service and religious goals, the more fundamental breach between the past and the present context of the religious life concerns its core spiritual meaning. The congregations flourished in a world that believed in a hierarchy of vocations – that is, that some callings in life were inherently superior to others – and in the conquest of the flesh as the means to achieve the higher levels. To put it in simple terms, the religious life was widely regarded as an elevated state raised on the three legs of poverty, chastity and obedience, and won enormous support and prestige in the Catholic world on that account. Since the Second Vatican Council enunciated the doctrine of the universality of vocations, the notion that any calling in life is inherently superior to another has been thrown into doubt – in the perceptions of the faithful if not in formal theology. More importantly, two of the three legs that raised the religious life above the ordinary state have collapsed. The ideal of poverty still holds an appeal, but in a post-Freudian world the suppression of sexuality seems unhealthy and psychologically violent, and in a world of democratic individualism the ideal of obedience hints of an abdication of the responsibility to evaluate and decide on moral issues for oneself.

In the light of the long Catholic tradition on humility and obedience as tools of spiritual perfection, Catherine McAuley may have believed that Bishop Cantwell's put-down of Mother M. Anne in Tullamore in connection with Fr Mathew might have benefited her spiritually and made her a better person. Such a view is totally foreign to present-day sensibilities. For women especially, it is now more likely to repel than attract. This is the fundamental problem now confronting the religious life. For all the respect, affection and gratitude that many of its practitioners have inspired in the Catholic faithful down through the years, there are things at its core that the world today finds alien and considers more likely to damage than uplift the human spirit. New forms of social action may disguise that fact. But in the long run the gaps and flaws that today's world would point to in the spiritual traditions from which the congregations emerged are proving to be fatally undermining to their popular appeal and evangelising impact. The challenge to generate a new and inspiring spirituality that would repair the defects of the old is thus more central to the future of the religious life than the demands of social radicalism.

9

Arriving Where We Started and Knowing the Place for the First Time

Teresa McCormack PBVM

John Weafer's research highlights a fascinating contrast in religious life in Ireland. On the one hand, there is a dramatic decline in the number of religious and an inevitable shift in their age profile. On the other hand, there is an optimism about the future and a belief that congregations can continue to make a contribution to Irish society, especially if they focus on some of the characteristics associated with their foundation (where they started). These characteristics include 'displaying a responsiveness to urgent societal needs which might not otherwise be met; working for the empowerment of poor and marginalised groups and, generally, being a counter-cultural voice and advocating a radical transformation of society' (CORI, 1997, a, p. 35).

The contrast outlined in the opening paragraph has been evident in congregations involved in education for some time and has, in fact, crystalised into a two-fold challenge to which most congregations are attempting to respond. That challenge was described in a 'Reflection Paper' by the Education Commission in 1997 and re-issued in 2001 as follows:

> Religious need to engage with others, in the task of developing new structures to take over the responsibilities for schools currently being held by them. Secondly, they need to identify new ways of being involved in education which will
>
> - enable unmet needs to be identified and responded to;
> - give rise to the empowerment of poor and marginalised groups;
> - represent a counter cultural voice promoting an alternative vision of society based on Gospel values (CORI, 1997, a, p.32).

I propose to devote the rest of this paper to elaborating on the two parts of the challenge and describing how congregations are responding. First, however, it is worth noting three sets of factors that provide the context in which the two-fold challenge emerged.

The Context for Change

The first set of factors in the changing context could be described as demographic and refers to the situation whereby the number of members of religious congregations is rapidly declining. The fact that, as Weafer's figures indicate, the number of religious working in education in 1999 is only just over 40% of the number working in education in 1989 is part of a well established trend. This trend can be seen clearly in official statistics and in the results of surveys conducted by the CORI Education Office in 1991 and 1997. The following statistics illustrate the changing demographics.

- In 1969/70 there were 2,300 religious working in secondary schools in the republic (34% of the teaching force); in

1998/99 there were 663 religious working in secondary schools (less than 6% of the teaching force).

- Throughout the 1990s, over twelve times as many religious retired from teaching as entered teaching.

- More than 40% of religious working in secondary schools are within ten years of compulsory retirement whereas less than 5% are aged under 35.

A second set of contextual factors relates to developments in the ways in which religious look at their own role in the Church and the wider society in which they work. This has led to a move by many religious from traditional to new ministries. Since the 1960s religious congregations have been seeking to rediscover their founding charisms and apply these to an analysis of the contemporary signs of the times. There is a growing consensus that the essential nature of religious life is its attempt to proclaim and give witness to a radically alternative way of life and vision of society based on the Gospel. This has led many congregations to engage in very searching evaluations of the appropriateness of their existing ministries and to face questions such as the following: is the fact that an apostolate is obviously a good work in itself a justification for our congregations continuing to do it in this place at this time? Is the societal need that moved us into these works many years ago still relevant? Is the counter-cultural stance that characterised the socially radical and politically subversive vision of the founders still operative?

The move to new ministries is reflected in the results of CORI's survey in 1991 and 1997. For example, it was found that

- of the religious who had left teaching posts before retirement age in previous years, about half did so in order to pursue new ministries. More than half of these ministries involved working with poor and marginalised groups;

- only a small minority (19%) of the ever declining number of newly professed members chose to work as teachers.

The third set of contextual factors has been the increased emphasis within the Church on promoting the involvement of lay people in a range of work previously reserved for religious and clergy. This has been particularly evident in schools. Therefore, apart from the declining membership of congregations, there is a strong case for the greater involvement by lay people in the running of schools. McCormack and Archer (1997) argued that 'there is no solid basis for believing that the continuation of Catholic education depends on the direct involvement of religious. The provision of Catholic schools is, in fact, the responsibility of the whole Catholic community. According to this kind of thinking, religious, having made a valuable contribution to establishing a network of Catholic schools, can move on to identifying and meeting urgent educational needs which cannot be met by others. Therefore, many religious believe that, even if the decline of membership of congregations was not taking place, it would be appropriate to begin to devise forms of trusteeship based on partnerships between congregations and others' (p. 4).

So far, I have been trying to suggest that issues about the involvement of religious in education illustrate a contrast or tension between attempts by congregations to rediscover their founding charism and apply it to contemporary society, on the one hand, and what they see as their responsibilities for their existing institutions on the other hand. The balance of the arguments would seem to suggest that congregations would be in a much better position to act in accordance with their founding charisms if they were free of many of their current responsibilities for schools. This would not mean that individual religious would not continue to work in schools endeavouring to carry out their work in a prophetic fashion. It would mean, however, that some of the financial and other resources that congregations devote to maintaining the present system could be redirected to identifying unmet needs, working with poor and marginalised groups and, generally, being a counter-cultural voice. In other words resources could be devoted to meeting the second part of the challenge that I mentioned at the beginning of the paper and to which I will return later.

In the next section the focus is on how congregations are responding to the challenge as it applies to their responsibilities for schools.

Transferring Responsibilities for Schools

A major part of the response to (a) the declining number of religious and, more importantly, (b) the need for increased lay involvement can be seen in the appointment of lay people as principals of schools and the establishment of Boards of Management. By the late 1990s the majority of secondary voluntary schools had lay principals and Boards of Management, the majority of whose members were lay. Despite these developments, religious congregations continue to have a substantial involvement in the ownership/trusteeship of schools. For example, religious congregations are the trustees of approximately 360 voluntary secondary schools attended by nearly 60% of the second-level, school-going population. A further 10% approximately of post-primary students are in 55 community schools in which religious congregations share trusteeship with the local Vocational Educational Committee. At primary level (where over 90% of the country's 3,200 national schools have a Catholic bishop as their patron) about 400 schools have religious congregations involved in trusteeship.

By the 1990s it had become clear that simply transferring roles such as school principal or manager to lay people would not respond adequately to the contextual factors highlighted earlier. As a result, attention has turned to finding ways of transferring the responsibilities associated with trusteeship to others, in ways that would ensure that the schools remained Catholic schools, retained their voluntary status and continued to value the congregation's philosophy and tradition. In the 1990s, significant work was done by religious congregations on clarifying the role of trustees and on ensuring that the importance of that role was recognised (see, for example, CORI, 1996; 1997, b). As a result, the role of the trustee in Irish education is being increasingly recognised. There is now a strong consensus that the most appropriate ways of accommodating the growing pluralism in society is through the availability of a diversity of school types. There is a commitment on the part of Government, arising from a corresponding concern in contemporary society to try to ensure that, as far as possible, parents will be able to choose schools that reflect their religious, ethical or cultural values. Trustees are crucial in ensuring that there is clarity about the philosophy and ethos that each school is trying to promote and between which parents can exercise their choice. For example, the White Paper in 1995 acknowledged the particular functions of trustees in relation to 'the continuity of the ethos of the school ... including a distinctive religious ethos' (p.146). The central role of trustees is also recognised in the Education Act (1998), especially in section 8 which deals with patrons.

Against this background, there is a commitment on the part of religious to set up systems and structures that will ensure a well planned transfer of trusteeship. Since 1994, CORI has been engaged in a systematic process of consultation and planning that included the publication of a handbook (CORI, 1996) and a review of options for the future of trusteeship (CORI, 1997, b). As part of that process, consideration was given to the possibility of transferring trusteeship to the diocese. Although it was recognised that this is a very attractive option in many circumstances, it is only rarely a realistic possibility for a variety of reasons. Arising out of these considerations, it was recognised that there is a strong need to develop new structures for Catholic Voluntary Schools in the future. This will involve Boards of Trustees, probably established under a Deed of Trust, taking over the functions currently performed by the leadership teams of congregations. The majority of members of these Boards of Trustees are likely to be lay people. A number of congregations have been exploring the possibility of setting up a single trust or Board of Trustees for all of their schools. Others are facing the challenge collaboratively by exploring the possibility of setting up a trust, probably on a regional basis, for the schools of the religious congregations in the region.

Among the matters currently being finalised are:

- the precise nature of the collaboration between congregations;
- the geographic unit in which collaboration might happen;
- legal instruments to underpin new structures such as Boards of Trustees;
- financial arrangements to sustain new structures into the future.

This work is now at an advanced stage and moving towards implementation. A consequence of the transfer of trusteeship would be the freeing up of congregations to focus on a new prophetic role in education. Aspects of that role are described in the next section.

A New Mission For Religious in Education

Earlier, I noted that many religious, who left posts in teaching, did so in order to work in new ministries more than half of which involved working with poor and marginalised groups (e.g. in adult and community education). This trend is reflected in Weafer's research. Thus adult education is one of only two areas where the number of religious involved actually increased from 1989 to 1999. Commenting on his table on education ministry, Weafer notes that 'Apart from the total reduction in the number of religious employed in the education ministry, the principal change in the statistical profile of this ministry is the movement away from the formal school setting to community, adult and third-level education'. In addition, it is likely that some of the shifts noted by Weafer, in relation to ministries other than education, also reflect the move away from teaching (e.g the increase in the number in social service ministry, especially community work and the fact that the numbers involved in the justice ministry has declined only slightly). In other words, it is likely that the availability of former teachers has enabled the involvement of religious in work with communities for social justice to be maintained and in some cases increased.

These findings support the view that while religious accept the inevitability of their withdrawal from schools, this does not mean that they have no further contribution to make to education. On the contrary, religious have recognised that questions about the future trusteeship of their schools represent only some of the strategic questions that they face. Thus, congregations are actively seeking new ways of bringing their perspective to bear on the educational enterprise. They know that, in the past, they performed a crucial role in the development of the education system and they believe that there are new urgent needs in education that they can meet or, at least, identify and highlight.

I mentioned earlier that many religious, in seeking new appropriate forms of involvement in education, are attempting to rediscover their founding charisms. For all of the indigenous congregations with a large involvement in education, the setting up of schools for Catholics represented a siding with those who were poor, marginalised and excluded. As we argued in the recent Summary & Guide to the Reflection Paper: 'The very act of giving as good an education as possible at first and second levels, was a defiance of the established colonial order, holding out the promise that those barred from all avenues of self advancement would be given the means to advance themselves. Thus religious sought not just to care for the marginalised and excluded, but, through the education they gave, they challenged the very institutionalised injustices that generated so much marginalisation' (CORI, 2001, p. 13).

The belief of religious in the nineteenth century that education could reduce or remove social inequality was a very radical one at the time. However, by the middle of the twentieth century, this belief had almost become a political orthodoxy and was the basis for major investment in education in many countries. Although this investment initially led to some reduction in inequality, it is now the case that the education system, albeit inadvertently, is one of the principal mechanisms by which inequalities are preserved from one generation to the next. This can be clearly seen from the fact that:

- more than 90% of the approximately 3500 young people who leave full-time education with no formal qualifications come from poor backgrounds and;

- an adult with no educational qualifications is nearly 9 times more likely to be poor than someone with third-level education.

These statistics, and many other similar ones that could be quoted, show quite clearly that it is not poor people who benefit from the education system. In other words, the education system, is to a large extent failing to meet the needs of poor people.

It is important to emphasise that the education system's failure to meet the needs of poor people is not primarily related to access. The Irish State is committed to providing school places free of charge to all young people up to and including Leaving Certificate level and subsidising places in third-level colleges. Therefore, unlike previous times in our history, religious can no longer be said to be responding to an unmet need, simply by making schooling available to children from poor families.

The reason why the education system is failing to meet the needs of poor people has been the subject of debate. In our work in CORI, we have identified a number of aspects of the system, as a whole, which we have argued contributes to the link between educational outcomes and poverty. These include curriculum and assessment, methods of allocating finance and the failure to adequately develop adult and community education (see, for example, CORI, 1998 & CORI, 1999). We have argued that the systemic nature of the continuing inequalities in the education system calls for a response that challenges the system itself and seeks to transform it.

Strategies for the Way Forward

In seeking out new ministries most congregations are likely to try to draw on their 'distinctive competencies'. In other words, in identifying a viable and meaningful role for themselves in the future, religious will try to draw on the educational insights and experience that has been built up over the last two centuries.

There are at least two parallels between present day Ireland and that of 200 years ago. First, Irish society is currently divided, not on denominational grounds, but on the basis of social class. These divisions are the result of past decisions about how, as a society, we chose to allocate our resources and, as CORI has been arguing, they reflect the prevailing vision and model of development. The second relevant parallel between the two Irelands is the emergence of an alternative vision of society or model of development, with which religious are increasingly identifying and which, indeed, they are playing a significant role in shaping. In the CORI 1997 Reflection Paper we argued that 'a further development of an alternative vision of society and, in particular, the identification of forms of education, which help promote this vision may be a focus for the future involvement of religious in education' (p. 36). We also emphasised, quoting Paulo Freire, that one of the most urgent unmet needs is for a form of community education that can be the 'means by which men and women deal critically and creatively with reality and discover how to participate in the transformation of their world' (CORI 1997, p. 44).

Against the background of some of the glaring injustices in the education system that have been identified by CORI and others, and the emerging alternative vision in Irish society, it seems to us that any new approach to mission and ministries must involve *political and social action* to challenge and change the education system and develop new educational responses that would contribute to making this alternative vision a reality.

At this stage, it is possible to identify a number of strategies that have emerged. All require significant shifts in the ways of thinking and working traditionally associated with religious. In particular, they require the adoption by religious of a new role in which they seek to exert *influence* rather than control, in which *collaboration* is a key ingredient and which has a strong *political* dimension. This new role is political in at least three inter-related respects:

1. It involves developing or supporting small scale initiatives that have social change among their objectives;

2. It involves participation in public debate, and;

3. It involves forming alliances with other groups motivated by similar values, particularly those drawn from marginalised sectors of society.

The term 'trail blazing' has been coined to describe a strategy that many religious are using in their efforts to give practical effect 'on the ground' to their radically alternative vision of society. It involves responding to the real need for empowerment of marginalised individuals and communities, not by setting up new institutions in religious ownership or management, but by participating with others in small pilot initiatives. There are hundreds of what might be termed 'pilot projects' in Ireland with which individual religious and their congregations are involved.

In relation to the second political dimension, namely participation in public debate, it is probably true to say that, in the past, religious and other Church-based groups tended to adopt a mainly reactive approach to public policy. Government policy initiatives were examined primarily with a view to identifying how they might affect 'our institutions' and then attempting to resolve any difficulties by means of private negotiations.

In recent years, however, a quite different approach has begun to be developed. Religious congregations, individually and collectively through CORI, have become increasingly involved in advocacy work that involves them outlining their vision of education, naming the values that support that vision, and promoting policies designed to make that vision a reality. This advocacy work has had some success in shaping education policy in areas such as educational disadvantage and adult and community education. Religious, through CORI, also had significant influence on the Education Act (1998). The 'ministry of influence' with regard to public policy is an increasingly important one for religious in relation to a growing number of national and international issues.

It is important to note that engaging in public debate is not an easy option. There are risks associated with an involvement in 'multilateral dialogue' that did not arise when 'bilateral negotiation' was the favoured approach. O'Brien (1994), in his book *Seeds of a New Church*, has addressed these risks in the following terms:

> 'This means the Church entering the public forum of debate, criticism, communication and advocacy as one participant among many, making its case on the moral authority of its praxis and not on the basis of institutional privilege... It means the courage to propose (the) Gospel as the basis of a true humanism, risking, on the one hand, rejection and, on the other, having its institutions and customs critiqued and reconstructed in the light of that reformulation of the Gospel'. (p. 20)

The recent efforts by religious to participate openly in public debate about education issues, on the basis of a Gospel-based vision, have sometimes been difficult and painful. They have seemed to open up divisions among the various Church-linked groups involved in education. In particular they have created tensions between those who have been given responsibility (often by religious themselves) for the task of protecting and promoting Catholic schools (e.g. management bodies) and those who are now attempting to act as an independent voice for religious and to look at the education system as a whole (e.g. CORI). Fortunately, in most cases, these tensions have been creative rather than destructive.

The third political dimension relates to forming alliances. Traditionally, religious in Ireland have undertaken their education apostolates alone. In general, congregations operated independently and such independence was greatly valued. There is now a growing recognition in religious life that independent action by congregations is becoming the exception rather than the rule. There is a new emphasis on collaboration among congregations in the first instance but, more importantly, between congregations and other groups in Church and society.

Conclusion

To respond to the twin challenges that I have been discussing in this paper will require what Fintan Sheeran (1993) calls 'mission reorientation'. In particular it will require a huge shift in the way that congregations approach their apostolic work. Religious will no longer be major providers of schooling within the existing system; rather they will be involved in critiques of that system and in pioneering innovative responses to unmet educational needs. In CORI, we have argued that mission reorientation cannot happen without *very radical organisational transformation* in relation to most aspects of the ways that congregations operate (structures, resources, leadership, etc.). For example, the 1997 Reflection Paper concluded that, in the relatively short period available, 'It is imperative that there is an organisational transformation, within congregations, so that concerns about past inheritance, including residual responsibilities for schools and other institutions, can be addressed while the congregation, as a whole, moves to wherever it can bring its charism to bear on responding to the most urgent needs of our times.' (p. 66)

In the last five or six years there has been significant movement by congregations in the direction advocated by the Reflection Paper. As I have tried to show, congregations are beginning to make progress in relation to preparing for the transfer of their schools to new forms of trusteeship. At the same time they are developing new ministries and are seeking to integrate these ministries within the congregation's overall mission and to ensure that there is corporate ownership of that overall mission. Some of these developments, within congregations, are reflected in the final section of John Weafer's report on trends in religious life. It is particularly worth noting the emphasis placed by congregational leaders on solidarity with poor people, collaboration and finding creative ways of applying their charisms. These were precisely the concerns of the founders of many congregations. Thus, in the words of T. S. Eliot,

We shall not cease from exploration
And the end of all our exploring
Will be to arrive where we started
And know the place for the first time.
'Little Gidding' from *Four Quartets* (1944)

References

CORI, *The Trusteeship of Catholic Voluntary Secondary Schools: A handbook for leaders of religious congregations,* Dublin: CORI Education Commission, 1996

CORI, *Religious congregations in Irish Education: A role for the Future? A Reflection Paper,* Dublin: CORI Education Commission, 1997a

CORI, *The Future of Trusteeship, A review of some options for the way forward,* Dublin: CORI Education Commission, (1997, b)

CORI, *Inequality in Education. The Role of Assessment and Certification,* Dublin: CORI Education Commission, (1998).

CORI, *Social Transformation and Lifelong Learning – Towards Policy on Adult and Community Education,* Dublin: CORI Education Commission, (1999)

CORI, *Religious Congregations in Irish Education: A Role for the Future? Summary and Guide to the Text,* Dublin: CORI Education Commission, (2001)

Education Act, 1998. Dublin: Government Stationery Office, December 23, 1998.

McCormack, T. and Archer, P. 'The Future of Trusteeship'. *The Future of Trusteeship: A review of some options for the way forward* Dublin: CORI Education Commission, 1997

O'Brien, Seeds of a New Church. Dublin: Columba Press, 1994

Sheeran, F., 'Struggling with renewal', *Religious Life Review* 32 pp. 85-92.

Charting our education future (White Paper), Dublin: Government Stationery Office, 1995